Rachel Wells is a mother, writer and cat lover. She lives in Devon with her family and her pets and believes in the magic of animals. Rachel grew up in Devon but lived in London in her twenties working in marketing and living in a tiny flat with an elderly rescued cat, Albert. After having a child, she moved back to Devon and decided to take the plunge and juggle motherhood with writing. *A Friend Called Alfie* is her sixth book.

Also by Rachel Wells:

Alfie the Doorstep Cat
A Cat Called Alfie
Alfie and George
Alfie the Holiday Cat
Alfie in the Snow

A Friend Called

ALFIE

RACHEL WELLS

avon.

Published by AVON
A division of HarperCollins*Publishers* Ltd
1 London Bridge Street
London SE1 9GF

www.harpercollins.co.uk

A Hardback Original 2019

First published in Great Britain by HarperCollins*Publishers* 2019

A catalogue copy of this book is available from the British Library.

ISBN: 978-0-00-835460-2

Typeset in Bembo 11.25/15 pt by Palimpsest Book Production Limited,
Falkirk, Stirlingshire
Printed and bound in the UK by CPI Group (UK) Ltd, Croydon CR0 4YY

MIX
Paper from
responsible sources
FSC
www.fsc.org
FSC™ C007454

This book is produced from independently certified FSC™ paper
to ensure responsible forest management.

For more information visit: www.harpercollins.co.uk/green

Acknowledgements

I can't believe I have written a sixth Alfie book – how wonderful. I feel so incredibly lucky to be able to still write about Alfie. And that is thanks to a lot of people:

Firstly, to the team at Avon: my editor Helen, Sabah in publicity, Dom in sales and the rest of the team who work so tirelessly on Alfie, from the page to the shelves. I love working with you and I love the Alfie Avon team!

Secondly, to my agents, Northbank Talent Management, who not only support me but also do a great job to getting Alfie out there to different parts of the world.

Thirdly, to my family and friends, who all help me with the writing process in their own ways. I appreciate each and every one of you. Special mention to Jessica, who this book is dedicated to – thank you for all the cat gifts that definitely inspire me.

And, lastly but very importantly, to my lovely readers who continue to buy my books, which enables me to keep writing them. I appreciate you all – those who follow me on social media, those who let me know that they enjoy the books, those who read quietly and especially those who share photos of their cats with me. Without you there would be no Alfie, so please appreciate how important you all are to me. I ran a competition to have a character named after a cat and, although I would have loved to use them all, I was limited to one – so a special mention to Janet Heath and her cat Oliver who appears in the book. I hope that you enjoy this latest Alfie offering and I hope you continue to follow me where ever you may be!

Facebook: https://www.facebook.com/acatcalledalfie/
Twitter: @ACatCalledAlfie
Instagram: rachelwellsauthor

For Jessica.

Chapter One

There was something about the Devon air, which felt so different from Edgar Road, where we lived most of the time in London. As the sea breeze whipped through my fur; it soothed and chilled me at the same time. It had been a very stressful time lately, and for my kitten George – who would probably argue that he was no longer a kitten but a proper cat – so we were enjoying a well-deserved holiday and a much-needed change of scene.

We were on a two week holiday at my human family's holiday home, Seabreeze Cottage, in Lynstow, Devon. The human family consisted of Claire, Jonathan, and their children Toby and Summer. Not forgetting our cat family; my cat son, George, and Gilbert, who lived full time at Seabreeze Cottage – Gilbert had been there before us and had become one of our closest friends. Although we didn't get to see him as often as we'd like, we always had fun whenever we were together. Gilbert was more independent than George and me, having fended for himself for years before we met him. If I'm honest, George and me are pampered cats, and I wouldn't have it any other way.

It hasn't always been that way, there was a time when I was homeless for a while, and I had to fend for myself. My first human owner, Margaret, died when I was a young cat, leaving me heartbroken and alone. I became a doorstep cat – a cat with different homes and owners – which comes with many benefits, I can assure you, but more of that later.

Thankfully, after some time on the streets, I found my way to Edgar Road, where I met my current human families. George came to live with my main human family as a kitten, having never had to fend for himself. He's a lot more spoilt than me, but he's kind-hearted, and I love him more than all the pilchards in the world.

We've had a rough year, my George and I. My girlfriend – the cat who George thought of as his mum – Tiger, had fallen ill and passed away before Christmas. We're still grieving her if I'm honest. I don't think you ever stop missing those you love, and I have loved and lost a lot in my life. But as a doorstep cat, with multiple humans in my life – Claire and Jonathan and their children Toby and Summer, Polly and Matt and their children Henry and Martha, Franceska and Tomasz and their children Aleksy and Tommy. You'll met my other humans soon enough.

Although this year was unfortunate in many ways, one thing we learnt was that life carries on regardless of the sadness you hold in your heart, and we had to carry on with it.

'I know, why don't we go to the sand dunes?' George suggested.

'Last one there's a dog,' Gilbert, who had joined us on the beach, shouted, taking off, we followed him, hot on his paws. I was breathless as I made it just a fraction later than George and Gilbert.

'Don't call me a dog,' I warned, narrowing my eyes and they both laughed.

'I'm going to slide down on my bottom,' George said, the carefree sound of his voice made me so happy. He wriggled

4

onto his bottom and tried to slide down the sand, the problem was that sand isn't very slippery, it's grainy, and it sticks to fur like glue. I went to try to give George a gentle push with my paw, but I tripped over his tail and landed with a bump almost on top of him.

'Yowl,' I cried.

'Dad,' he chastised as we both started rolling down, and although it was a little bit scary, we got to the bottom in one piece.

'That was so much fun, Dad,' George said, reminding me that maybe he was growing up fast, but he was still a kitten, my kitten, in so many ways. 'Can we do it again?'

'Let me catch my breath,' I pleaded, I certainly wasn't a kitten in any way anymore, but I would do anything for my boy.

'Come on, George,' Gilbert shouted from the top. 'Let Alfie recover. I'll roll down with you, it did look like fun after all.'

We spent the rest of the evening playing, rolling and enjoying the beach, finding some much-needed peace. It became another evening for us to feel lucky about.

It wasn't just George and me who needed a break in Devon, my human family did too. Jonathan had recently got a promotion at work, which is a good thing, but it meant he would have to work longer hours, and harder than he had before. Claire had told him to go for the job, but she was also worried about what it would mean for us as a family. She had to be supportive, however, because we all knew that Jonathan was only doing it for us, to provide more pilchards for George and me – yum – good schools for the children (whatever that meant) and Claire was even getting a new car. So this much-needed holiday had brought us all together in a way that reminded us that we were a loving family. Not without our problems, of course, but there is no such thing as a problem-less family, another thing I had learned the hard way. And when I heard Jonathan and Claire talking at night when the children were asleep, I knew they were both slightly nervous about how the new job would be and how they were going to cope with not having Jonathan around so much. I tried not to worry about them, but it wasn't easy – I worried about everyone I loved.

During the holiday, Claire, Jonathan and the children had enjoyed picnics on the beach, walks, and bike rides. George had tried to go join them in the bike basket, but he kept falling onto the handlebars of Toby's bike, so Claire had banned him. While they had their human adventures, we had our own feline ones. Gilbert was quite an active cat, he often took us on what he would call country walks. They were more like runs, through fields – the first time we came here we were cornered by a herd of sheep and barely got out with one of our lives intact. He and George climbed trees while I stayed safely on the ground, and of course, we visited the beach, but mainly in the evenings when we had it to ourselves. After losing Tiger, I didn't realise how much I needed a change of scene. Claire said Devon was like a tonic, and she wasn't wrong – I felt as if I could breathe properly for the first time since I lost her.

In the evenings at the cottage, Claire cooked, Jonathan relaxed, the children, worn out by the activities slept well. Sometimes the neighbours came round, or someone would babysit for us while Claire and Jonathan went to the local pub. We were quite friendly with some of the other families in the village, Seabreeze had become a home from home. Even the next door neighbour, Andrea, who once tried to run us out of the village, was our friend now. It's a long story which culminated in Seabreeze Cottage almost being set on fire, but luckily Gilbert and I foiled the plan and saved the day. It's what I did. As I said it's a very long story but Andrea, who had been deserted by her husband, now had a new man friend called Fred, who was very jolly, and everyone agreed he made Andrea a lot more likeable. It's a shame the same couldn't be said for her cat, Chanel. Chanel was George's first crush, she was a mean, unfriendly cat, and George's devotion to her had been quite alarming. Luckily he had moved on now and saw her for the scowling cat she was. Despite the family being friends of ours now, Chanel still hissed at us whenever she saw us. Not everyone is kind, unfortunately, and not everyone wants to be a good friend. I am, George is, my humans are, but Chanel certainly isn't. Thankfully George has learnt to give her a wide berth, and her hiss is definitely worse than her bite – not that we ever get close enough to test that theory.

'Right, it's getting late, we should be getting home before Claire worries,' I said, worn out from rolling and covered in sand.

'OK, but we can come and play this again, can't we?' George asked.

'If you're good,' Gilbert replied, giving me a blink.

'I might need a day or two to recover,' I said. 'I'm not as young as you, George.'

'No, but you're not old either,' he replied quickly. Gilbert and I exchanged a glance. Since losing Tiger, George was worried about losing me too. It was only natural but I wasn't going anywhere. There were plenty of lives left in this cat yet.

'Oh there you are boys,' Claire said, when we walked into the kitchen, having done our best to get the sand off us and failed, as usual. When we went back to London from Seabreeze, the sand had a habit of coming back with us.

'Meow,' I said in greeting before the three of us headed over to our food bowls to eat our supper.

'Right, well Jonathan and I are about to settle down to watch a film if you want to join us?' she said. I loved how Claire always spoke and treated us as if we were humans. We were cleverer than most humans, but I appreciated the gesture anyway.

'Meow,' I said. Snuggling up on the sofa in front of a film sounded the perfect way to end the day.

We ate, cleaned up and headed into the small TV room. Gilbert took his spot on his favourite chair while George and I curled up in the middle of the sofa – the comfiest place.

'Blimey, Claire, there's barely any room for us, these cats take up all our space,' Jonathan said as he squeezed himself into the small space we'd left for him.

'But, darling, we wouldn't have it any other way,' Claire replied, kissing him on the cheek and trying to move us. George and I pretended to be asleep, so in the end, she had no choice but to sit on the floor in front of her husband.

Chapter Two

'Back to Edgar Road, tomorrow, son,' I said, trying to hide my sadness that our holiday in Lynstow was coming to an end. I loved being here; I enjoyed the change of scene, especially getting to see Gilbert, I loved how relaxed my family seemed, not to mention the beach. I even quite liked sand now. Actually no, I tolerated sand but I struggle with the way it sticks to my fur like glue and makes grooming such hard work. But then I loved watching the sunset, and the soothing sound of the waves gently lapping the shore, so perhaps I'll just have to put up with sand.

'I know, Dad, and I'm glad to be going back, to see our friends and especially Hana, but I'll miss it here, and I'll miss Gilbert of course.'

'Me too, but we'll be back before you know it.' All our families from London had pledged to come to holiday here together at some point and being here with all of them was one of my favourite times ever. Having everyone I love under one roof made me feel like the luckiest cat alive. Sure the cottage would be quite crowded, noisy and chaotic, but I wouldn't want it any other way.

'But,' George paused, looking a little upset. 'This will be the first time we go back to Edgar Road and not see Tiger mum.' His voice cracked, I could feel his pain. I nuzzled him, reassuringly.

'I know, son,' I said. Gilbert looked over at me and gave

me a reassuring blink. 'It'll be strange not going back and telling her all about our holiday, but we can still tell her.'

The memory brought back the pain I felt every time I would walk past Tiger's house, like I was being stabbed in the heart. There were times I would wait for her by the cat flap, even though I knew she'd never come out of it again – the sorrow hadn't abated. It was hard, but as the grown-up, it was my duty to step up and help him through his grief.

I learnt that you can't protect your children from loss; you can't keep all the bad in the world away from them. However, you can do your best to help them cope with bumps in the road, it's all any parent can do. Becoming a parent makes you realise how much capacity you have for love, but it also shows you your limitations. No matter how hard you try, you can't control what the world will send your way.

The night was drawing in on our final holiday evening, and I thought about all those I had loved and lost. The pain doesn't get any easier, but you do get used to it a bit more, I guess.

'George, do you remember the first time we had to go past her house knowing she wasn't there?'

'Yes, I do, it was horrible in so many ways.'

'What about the second time, when she wasn't there at Christmas?'

'It was difficult.'

'I know, but what I want you to know is that it gets a little easier each time,' I said with the authority of someone who knew this to be true.

'But doesn't that mean we don't love her anymore?' he asked.

'No, it means we love her just as much as ever, but we also accept that we have to get used to her not being there,' I tried to explain.

'You know.' Gilbert spoke for the first time in ages. 'Missing someone is natural. George, I miss you when you're not here in Lynstow, but I have to get on with life, and sometimes when I miss you, I just think of something you said, or when you made me laugh, and I feel better. I almost feel you here with me.'

I felt choked with emotion at Gilbert's words.

'I think of Tiger mum all the time.'

'Look, George,' I said, hopping on my paws excitedly as the stars began to appear in the sky. 'Look at that bright star. What do you see?'

'It's her, I just know it,' George said, sounding happier. 'I can tell her all about how we've had a lovely holiday now.' I nodded as he proceeded to do so. Gilbert and I looked on, giving him a bit of space to talk to his mum in the sky. I tried not to get caught up in the unfairness of it all. I still hadn't accepted why she had to be taken from us, but I also knew that overcoming my own issues was part of process too, but something I felt I had to keep hidden from George. No yowling for this cat, at least not until I was alone.

'You know we are lucky,' I said, trying to keep my voice steady, as George finished speaking.

'We are,' Gilbert said.

Gilbert came to live in Seabreeze Cottage after running away from his home. I learnt that not every human was kind to their pets and I felt so sorry for him when I first heard his story, but at least now he had us, and he loved his life here. We tried to get him to come and live in London with us, but he said he wouldn't be able to live away from the sea. I could almost understand that, but I loved London too. I loved the traffic and the bustle, and of course, London was where my other friends and families lived too.

'We're lucky that we get to spend time here, together,' George said. 'And I'm lucky to have such good families and friends. Not to mention how blessed I am to be such a handsome and charming cat who everyone loves.' George winked with his right eye.

'Chip off the old block that one,' Gilbert said, with a grin.

I had no idea what he meant.

Packing up the cottage was always a bit of a frantic time. Not for George and me – we did very little but watch on as Jonathan moaned about how much stuff Claire had brought. He would grumble 'how on earth am I supposed to fit it in the car' although he always did. George and I would sit on the lawn and watch him huffing and puffing and saying words that no child or cat should hear, sweat rolling down his face in the sun as he tried to get all the suitcases into the boot of the car. While he was doing that, Claire would be tidying the place. Although there was a caretaker at Seabreeze who cleaned the place and fed Gilbert, Claire wouldn't dream of her thinking she was above cleaning her own house. So she whipped through the house from top to bottom while the children got to play with their friends for the last time.

Gilbert had made himself scarce. We said goodbye to him that morning as we had a last walk before our long journey home. He didn't actually like to see us go, he said it made him sad, so he would always disappear just before we were

14

setting off. He was a softy at times, despite the fact that he was a survivor cat, who proved to be made of sterner stuff than many. I would miss him. But I knew we'd see him again soon. And as I felt sad I remembered how lucky I was to have so many friends and such good ones at that.

Once the house was emptied of our stuff, Claire, as usual, had to check the house again before she was satisfied we hadn't left anything behind. Jonathan would surely moan about the traffic they were bound to hit if we didn't get moving soon. They rounded up the children who were tearful at having to say goodbye to their summer holiday. Claire jollied them along by reminding them they were going to see their friends at home soon, and George and I were put into our car carrier, which I didn't love to be honest. Although George and me were in it together, and there was a soft blanket for us to lie on, I wasn't a fan of feeling caged. It made me a bit anxious, not that I'd let on to George. It was a shame, I thought, as I hid my feelings that Jonathan didn't do the same.

'Claire, if we don't get going soon I'm going to be driving for hours and hours longer than necessary,' he snapped.

'OK, keep your hair on, we're ready. Toby, strap yourself in,' she commanded as she strapped Summer into her car seat. Toby was old enough to do it himself. Finally, after going back to check the house one last time, Claire got into the car.

'Right, can I leave now?' Jonathan asked, sounding tetchy.

'Yes, is everyone alright?'

'I'm hungry,' Summer said, and the long journey home began.

It was nightfall by the time we reached Edgar Road.

Jonathan was right, the traffic had been terrible, but Claire managed to entertain him by asking him crossword clues. I learnt that if Jonathan felt clever he was happy, so I think Claire only asked him clues she knew he'd know the answer to. She was quite intelligent, my Claire. The children were given snacks, and finally, they fell asleep, which meant the journey was long but peaceful. Even George slept gently beside me. I was desperate to stretch my legs and get some fresh air. As Claire got the children into the house and Jonathan took the luggage out, letting George and me out first, I breathed the London air, so different from Devon but so familiar.

'Welcome home, son,' I said as George and I stretched. Before we went into the house, I allowed myself a quick glance towards where Tiger used to live. No, it wasn't easier yet, but I hoped that it would before too long as I swallowed back a yowl.

When Tiger was alive the first thing I would have done after a holiday was to have gone to see her, and tell her how glad I was to be home. But I couldn't do that now, I couldn't tell her how much I'd missed her, and it pained me to have to turn away from her house, knowing she was no longer there.

I blinked away a tear, ushered my son inside the house and stepped into the warmth of home. Once in the kitchen, I prepared to settle him down for the night, it had been a long and tiring journey. Frankly I just wanted to forget everything and sleep, hoping tomorrow I would wake up feeling better, or at least ready for a new day.

Chapter Three

The week after getting back from Devon, I developed post-holiday blues. Jonathan had to go straight back to work to start his new job. Overnight the relaxed – well for Jonathan anyway – holiday Jonathan was replaced by an even more stressed out one than usual. Claire had to get the children ready to start school again – buying uniforms, shoes and bags and organising clubs; it was a flurry of activity for everyone. But I felt flat, and although I got to see my other humans and cat friends, I still couldn't quite shake the gloom.

It didn't help that London was greyer than Devon and I was feeling more than a little bit down in the dumps. I kept telling George that our grief over Tiger would get easier, but it wasn't feeling that way at the moment. Seeing our cat friends on Edgar Road – Rocky, Elvis, Nellie, and even the sour-faced Salmon – couldn't cheer me up. My paws felt heavy as I walked, although I knew I needed to snap out of it, I had no idea how. Being a cat wasn't always as easy as people thought.

I did, thankfully, have a bit of time to myself to try to let out my sadness, which I could only do alone. George was next door with his best friend Hana, a lovely cat who moved here from Japan last year. Hana was about the same age as George, and she was 'Mikeneko' which means she had a coat of three colours, in English, we would say Tortoiseshell. She was beautiful and sweet, one of the calmest cats I'd ever met – quite the opposite to my boy. I did wonder if George and

Hana were more than friends, after all the boy was growing up. George could act a bit like a teenager when I asked him about Hana – he would shut me down pretty quickly, and say they were just good friends. His reluctance just made me want to know more . . .

However, they did adore each other regardless of their relationship status, and they saw one another most days. Hana had been a house cat in Japan and didn't go out, something that both horrified and fascinated me. Since being in London, we had managed to get her out a bit, but she preferred being indoors. It was her choice, and I understood that it took all sorts of cats to make the world go round.

Hana lived next door to us with Sylvie and her teenage daughter Connie. Connie was the girlfriend of my first human child friend, Aleksy, who I had known almost from the first day I arrived at Edgar Road. I couldn't believe he was a teenager now, my child friends were growing up fast. Aleksy and Connie had a sweet relationship, a lot of hand-holding and blushes. However, they were both clever children, and so I personally thought they were a good match.

Also, Sylvie was now seeing one of our other friends, Marcus, which made her happy. I had to admit she was a bit unstable when she first moved here, and she had me a little worried. She'd been through a horrible divorce, so it was understandable. She was lonely and missing her home in Japan. I knew how hard starting over could be, after all, I had done it. But lately, she smiled a lot. Also, she always gave us fresh fish when we visited which obviously helped. We all met Marcus through his father, Harold, who happens to be one of George's best human friends. George and I saved his life last year when he was ill, and since then he's become part of our family.

We know so many people, I know, it's hard to keep track of them all, but that is what a doorstep cat does, and I'm very good at it if I do say so myself.

Perhaps the reason I was feeling glum was because I was feeling a bit left out. Everyone was in love, or at least it seemed that way, apart from me, who had lost the only two cat women I had ever loved. Snowball, my first love moved away with her family a few years back, and you all know about Tiger. Goodness, I really was feeling sorry for myself.

I didn't usually wallow in self-indulgence, but today I was letting myself feel my feelings. So I curled up on Jonathan's favourite cashmere blanket, which I am absolutely not allowed anywhere near, under any circumstances, and had a little therapeutic cat nap.

George woke me, bounding up to me excitedly and then sitting on my tail. He was a little bit clumsy sometimes, my boy.

'Hey,' I said, stretching my paws out and yawning.

'Claire just came home with Toby, Summer, Henry and Martha and said that Polly was coming round in a bit with a surprise for us all.' His eyes were wide with excitement. 'I think that includes us, Dad.'

Since Jonathan had secured his big promotion, Claire had given up her part-time job so she could spend more time with the children. Polly worked irregular hours sometimes and Matt was quite busy, so Claire said she was a bit like their part-time nanny. Claire also looked after Harold, George's old man friend who lived at the end of Edgar Road, Marcus' father. She did his shopping and dropped in on him regularly making sure he ate a good lunch. Marcus lived with him and took care of him, but he had to work, and of course he also had Sylvie, so Claire helped out there a lot. She loved looking after people – and cats – and she was very good at it. Mind you, I think she learnt a lot of her skills from me.

'A surprise, you say?' I narrowed my eyes. 'Do you think it's food?'

'I don't know, but Claire said that Polly had sworn her to secrecy, the children are excited, and I'm hoping that it might be something for all of us, we should go downstairs so we don't miss it.' George hopped around excitedly, catching my tail yet again.

'Yowl! George, you need to be more careful,' I gently chastised. I knew he wouldn't be, he never was. 'Did you have a nice afternoon?' I asked, thinking I may get to find out a little more about his feelings for Hana. 'With Hana,' I added.

'Yes, I'll tell you about it later, but come on, let's go now otherwise we'll never find out what this surprise is.

'What on earth is that?' George asked as eyes wide we stared at something wriggling in Polly's arms.

'I have never seen anything like it,' I said. It was tiny. Smaller than George had been as a kitten. We all peered in, the thing was a light brown colour, with a dark brown snout and dark brown tips to his ears.

'It's a puppy!' Martha shouted, going to her mum and trying to reach for it. George and I exchanged a glance. Surely not? They wouldn't . . . Polly bent down.

'Yes, it's a puppy, but he's very little, so we need to be

22

gentle, and we also need to make sure that we don't scare him by being too loud.' The children crowded around.

'Whose puppy is it?' Summer asked, suspiciously.

'Well, Summer, he is going to live with us at our house,' Polly said. 'But when I'm at work, he'll be here with Claire, and with you guys when you get back from school, so in a way, he's all of ours.'

'A bit like Alfie and George?' Toby asked. He was a bright boy.

'Exactly.'

'What's his name?' Henry asked.

'We don't have one yet, love,' his mum replied. 'So this afternoon we should all think of a name for him. He's a pug by the way.'

'Yay.' The children all started throwing out suggestions and George and I backed away into the kitchen.

'Puppy,' Summer shouted.

'Nah that's boring,' Henry replied.

'Flower,' Martha suggested.

'But he's a boy,' Toby pointed out.

'Spiderman,' Henry shouted.

'Don't be silly,' Summer replied.

George and I left them to it.

'Is this what I think it is?' George asked, sounding horrified.

'What do you think it is?' I asked.

'A dog, they got a dog.'

'I'm afraid it seems as if they have. Although it's quite a strange-looking dog. And small, but it'll probably grow a bit like you did.' I couldn't believe Polly would betray us like this. Who on earth got a dog when there were two perfectly good cats around?

'And they said this dog will be at our house a lot,' George said. 'This cannot be happening. It's the worst thing in the world.' He put his head in his paws. I have to admit I felt like doing the same, but I had a feeling that this puppy was here to stay, and therefore, I had quite a lot of sorting out to do.

I've never been a dog fan, Tiger and I used to tease dogs on leads by getting them to chase us and sit just out of reach so they couldn't get us — it was just so much fun. Although I have been chased by a dog or two in my time, I have never let one catch me. I always outsmart them. But I digress. The problem is that I think of dogs as being like cats but without the brains, which is why they don't get to be independent the way we cats are. Perhaps my prejudice wasn't a good thing to pass onto George. Because by the sounds of it, this puppy was going to be at our house a lot and I knew that we needed to be friends with it, I mean him. We couldn't be mean, that wasn't what we did. And the humans seemed to like him, so we had to too. It might not be easy, but we would have to do our best.

'George, I might not be a fan of dogs, but I have to be honest with you, I haven't actually spent any quality time with one.'

'What? Never?'

'Nope, and I don't actually personally know any dogs,' I explained.

'So why do you say they are all terrible?' George asked, eyes wide.

'Um, good question. Sometimes we judge things before we really know them, I may have done that with dogs.' I was desperate to limit any damage before George traumatised the very tiny dog. 'I think it's just a cat and dog thing, we are different from them, and that's OK. This puppy, he's a baby, we need to give him a chance.' I wasn't sure if I was making any sense, but this was a new side of me. I was being forced to turn my long-held convictions on their head. That wasn't going to be easy.

'So you mean this dog might be OK?' He didn't sound convinced, but then neither was I.

'He might be, in fact, I'm sure he will be. Remember how we try to get everyone to be friends, well in this case that includes the puppy dog, I'm afraid.' I had a feeling I wasn't doing the best job ever. But this was a new situation for me.

'Um, so I shouldn't hiss at him? Or try to scratch him.'

'No, George.' Something occurred to me. 'The thing is that he's clearly a baby and he's come to live with Polly and family, the way you came to live with us as a tiny kitten and that was quite frightening in the early days wasn't it?'

'Yes, and when Toby came to live with us he was frightened too wasn't he?' George had many faults, but he was a very perceptive lad. Toby was adopted by Claire and Jonathan a few years back. Now it seemed as if he had always been here with us, but it had been hard for him at first.

'This dog might be feeling frightened and we must be superior cats to make sure he's alright.' I had always tried to impart that kindness was the most important thing we could do for one another.

'Alright, Dad, in this case, I will do so but also if he does turn out to be the way you say dogs can be I can't guarantee that I'll be nice to him forever.'

'That sounds reasonable and fair, George,' I said. I hoped this puppy might prove me wrong about dogs. I'm not sure I felt that optimistic, though. But even I, faced with one of my long-held views, was questioning myself.

Claire came into the kitchen, clutching the puppy to her chest. He was tiny and had quite short legs. Even though I wasn't sure how big he would grow to be, I desperately hoped he wouldn't grow too big. Big dogs definitely scared me if they got too close.

'Alfie, George, come and meet our new friend,' she said, gently, moving towards us and kneeling down.

George and I exchanged glances as we tentatively moved nearer. I had never seen a dog like this up close before. He was calmer now and, as we peered at him, the little dog put his tongue out and licked his nose. Then he seemed to focus on us, with his big eyes, but it was hard to tell what he was thinking. Just then he gave a little wag of his short tail which sort of stuck to his bottom.

'Oh goodness, he already likes you!' Claire exclaimed. 'Welcome to the family, and Alfie, George, it's time for you to formally meet Pickles. The children voted and this name, which was Polly's idea, actually won.'

Really? Just as I thought it couldn't get any worse. Pickles? What kind of name was that? Even for a dog.

Chapter
Four

It was Monday, our first day alone with Pickles the pug. We'd locked eyes with him a lot, but not one of the children let him out of their sight. They really did seem to adore him, which put George's nose out of joint a bit. Being usurped by a dog was pretty low.

Claire had given us a bit of a lecture this morning, because Pickles was coming to our house and would be left alone with us while Claire took the children to school. She wasn't ready to take him on the school run, but said she would be doing so when he was a bit bigger. What this had to do with us, I had no idea, but we listened. Or I did, George was cleaning his paws and sulking.

She went on to share that our new 'friend' Pickles was two months old. He was supposed to go to a family, but something happened, and they couldn't have him at the last minute. Someone Polly worked with asked her if she knew anyone who wanted an adorable pug puppy, and Polly knew Matt had always wanted one. I was still coming to terms with the fact the children had been asking for a puppy (how dare they?), as it would also mean they had a pet who lived with them. I suppose, we visited often but didn't live there, so Polly and Matt decided we all had a share in a puppy. Hmm.

Not one to keep things succinct, Claire told us that Pickles was allowed outside, because he had been to the vet. Apparently, he'd had the right injections, but he mustn't go out on his own because he was a dog, not a cat. Not that we needed reminding of that. So, she was asking us to stay in with Pickles until she got back from the school run, rather than go into the garden or for our usual early morning walk. Torture for a doorstep cat. Finally, she finished talking just as the doorbell went and we opened it to find Polly, Henry and Martha stood on our doorstep. Henry was holding Pickles.

Polly rushed off as she was running late, the children all crowded around Pickles in the hallway, fussing him. George looked at me.

'Is he going to take all the attention off me forever?' George sounded horrified.

'Of course not, he's a novelty right now but what do I always tell you? There's enough love to go round.'

'Um, maybe, but I am so much cuter than him.' George stomped his paw.

'Of course you are, George.'

George was so used to being the centre of attention, and now there was a new pet on the block. This might not be as straightforward as I thought. Actually, I never thought it would be straightforward, but this was threatening to be more of a nightmare than I imagined.

'Hello,' I said, unsure if he would be able to understand me when George, Pickles and I were finally alone.

'Are you my new friends?' Pickles asked.

'Yes, I suppose we are your new friends,' I replied. He sounded young, and if I was honest, when he looked at me with his big eyes, he was quite adorable. But George was still sulking, I'm not sure he agreed.

'I'm happy to meet you both,' Pickles said. 'It's scary living with a new family, but everyone seems so nice,' he mouthed, as he ran around in a circle. Why can't puppies stay still?

'What are you doing?' George asked, scowling in Pickles' direction.

'I'm trying to catch my tail,' Pickles replied.

He might get smarter as he got older, I thought, and tried to convey this to George through my glare.

'So are you settling in well?' I asked. It still felt a bit awkward, although it was easier to talk to him now he was no longer running in circles.

'Yes, I cried a bit last night because I felt lonely. Henry convinced Polly that I could sleep on his bed, so I snuggled up to him, and that wasn't quite so bad.'

'You like to talk,' George pointed out.

'Be nice,' I whispered to George.

'Welcome to Edgar Road,' George said, not exactly sounding welcoming.

'And we both arrived here on our own at different points. So you know, if you feel a bit down, you can talk to us,' I said, more kindly.

'Thank you, I think I'm going to like it here,' Pickles said. Then he sat down and smiled at us with his wrinkly face.

'Dad, can I go out?' George asked.

'We're supposed to be looking after Pickles,' I pointed out.

'But I told Hana I'd go and see her this morning.' Although Hana didn't go out much, she had a cat flap, so George visited her regularly, as did I sometimes. I didn't want to force him to stay and help me with Pickles as he'd probably end up resenting me for it, so I thought I'd be best off letting him go. Although, I would have liked to go out . . .

'OK, I can take care of Pickles, but you need to get used to him because he's going to be here a lot,' I whispered to George, as we moved towards the back door.

'Fine, and I will be nice, but now I would rather be with my actual friend.' George sounded a bit surly; he was still a little put out at how the children ignored him as soon as Pickles arrived on the scene. It was jealousy, something that siblings often suffered from. Goodness, get me I was already thinking of him as if he was part of the family, which was very magnanimous of me if I did say so myself.

'But give Pickles a chance, George, after all he might be a bit like a brother to you now.'

'Well perhaps, seeing as you are so keen to adopt the puppy, you might tell him not to eat your food,' George snapped before he disappeared out of the cat flap. I turned to see Pickles, nose deep in my breakfast.

'Pickles, that food is not for you, it's for cats,' I said, trying not to sound angry. I had been saving that, though, so now I'd be hungry later.

'I thought it tasted a bit funny. Never mind, can we go and play now?'

Oh goodness, I thought, here I was yet again in the role of reluctant parent. Why did this keep happening to me?

I was so pleased to see Claire when she came home that I ran straight into her legs and gave them a welcoming rub. I was also happy to see that she had Sylvie with her.

Pickles had been very busy, exploring the house; he had tried to get into every cupboard, thankfully he didn't succeed. Finally he found some food that the kids had dropped under the kitchen table, which he ate despite me telling him not to before he ran into a door. He was clearly in the learning stage of life, and only at the very beginning. After he'd eaten, he then ran up and down the kitchen for no apparent reason before jumping into the dog bed that Claire had put in the corner for him.

'Are you alright?' I had asked. He was breathing quite heavily and making a snorting, or snuffling noise.

'I have had so much fun with you this morning, Alfie, but I'm tired now so I might just close my eyes.' As he had drifted off to sleep, I thought about joining him, I was so exhausted.

'Oh my goodness he's so cute,' Sylvie said, picking him out of his bed and giving him a cuddle. I kind of understood how George felt, as I became invisible.

'Isn't he? The kids love him, and Polly is besotted. I think she wanted a third child, but Matt put his foot down, so Pickles has taken that place.'

'Makes sense. I've always been more of a cat person myself, but he is adorable. Look at that little face.' As Pickles wiggled into Sylvie's arms, Claire gave me a head scratch.

'Where's George?' she asked me.

'Meow,' I replied.

'He's at ours,' Sylvie replied, 'he came in just before I bumped into you.'

'Right, shall I put the kettle on?' Claire said.

'Please, I'd love a coffee, but then I'm not sure I can bear to pull myself away from Pickles to drink it.'

'Honestly, everyone adores him. But then we have to make sure Alfie and George don't feel left out,' Claire said. Ah, so someone had noticed us after all. I purred with pleasure.

'Claire, you treat those cats as if they're your children sometimes.'

'They are.' Claire shrugged and I purred in agreement.

'So how are things with Marcus?' Claire asked, and I settled down to listen to the latest news.

'Good, we're taking it slowly, what with all we've both been through, but it's nice having him live so near, and he's such a good man. Also, he grounds me, stops me from my you know, my darker thoughts, I guess.'

'I heard a whisper that Harold thinks you are wonderful,' Claire said with a laugh.

'From Harold, that is a huge compliment,' Sylvie laughed. Harold could be very grumpy but a bit like a chocolate, despite the hard exterior he had a soft centre.

'And speaking of Harold, I have to go and see him in a bit, shall I take you, Pickles?' Claire asked.

'Woof,' Pickles replied, and I knew that although he had no idea who Harold was, he very much wanted to go and I would be able to have a luxurious rest on my own.

Chapter
Five

After a frankly exhausting time with Pickles the pug, I went out to see if any of my friends were about. I hoped to bump into George who seemed to be giving the house a wide berth. I needed to talk to him because Pickles needed us, both of us, and I needed George to see that. I also could have used the help, having been run ragged by the puppy. And it was only day one.

I understood George had mixed feelings. Not only had I always told him to avoid dogs, but he was now supposed to accept someone into his life, his family, that he was unsure of.

I padded over to the area where we cats often hang out, sort of our recreation ground on Edgar Road. Nellie was there, lying near a bush, and Elvis was nearby playing with some leaves. I joined them.

'Hey, Alfie,' they both greeted me.

'Have you seen George?' I asked.

'He came by earlier and said that he was going to see Harold.'

'Right, and did he tell you about the puppy?' I asked.

'Yes, and I got the impression he's not too impressed,' Nellie said. 'He said that dogs are dumb and he shouldn't have to be nice to it.'

'Pickles, not it,' I said. 'Goodness, this might be worse than I thought. I was afraid that this might happen, but Pickles is just a baby, and it looks like he's a full member of the family now. They're not going to give him back after all. And I wouldn't want that to happen to any pet.'

'A dog, in a cat's world,' Elvis mused.

'What am I going to do? I've always been against dogs, but now I am babysitting one! Anyway, I like him, and I need to find a way to get George to do the same.'

'Your life is always getting complicated, isn't it?' Nellie pointed out. She was right, it was. And now there was Pickles.

'The lad is still hurting about Tiger, and now there's yet another change in his life.' Elvis could be a very wise cat when the mood took him.

'I know, so I can't be too demanding, but I think I need to get him to at least tolerate Pickles sooner rather than later. He's going to be at our house a lot, and I don't want George to go out every time he comes.' I felt a shudder run through my fur at the thought of me having to babysit the dog alone. I didn't want Pickles to come between us. 'And when he's a bit older we can probably go out and leave him. Or maybe Claire will take him with her more, dogs tend to go out with humans a lot, so it's just in the short term. Hopefully.' The idea that I could sell this to George cheered me.

'Exactly, Alfie, this dog is now part of the family, so maybe you should just get George to think of him as his little brother and teach him what he knows,' Nellie said.

'What?' I was confused.

'Well, if they brought another kitten in he might be a bit jealous at first, but then you'd say he was a big brother and he had to teach the kitten to cat, so why don't you give him that role with Pickles?'

'You know, Nellie, you might have something there. I'll

38

tell him he's a big brother now with responsibility, and if he teaches Pickles all he knows—' I paused and tried not to think of all the scrapes George got himself in '—then he might accept him more readily. You guys are amazing, thank you. And where's Rocky?'

'Oh he was tired, so he went off for a nap. That cat likes its sleep.'

'What cat doesn't?' I replied.

George appeared shortly afterwards, saving me from having to go and find him.

'How was Harold?' I asked. Harold and George shared a love of digestive biscuits, among other things. Harold dunked them in strong tea, until they were soggy and then fed them to George.

'He was fine, good actually. It's nice and quiet at his house. Not like ours,' George replied in that stroppy way of his when he was sulking. 'Although Claire took Pickles to see him earlier and even he said the dog was sweet.' He stomped his paw.

'George, I know you're not happy about Pickles, but I need you to help me,' I started, carefully.

'Help you do what?' George asked, sounding surly.

'George, when you came to live with me, I was your dad straight away, and you were so tiny, there was so much for me to teach you.'

'So?' Gosh this boy could act like a teenager at times.

'Well, you had me, and our cat friends, and Tiger mum to help you learn as you grew, so that made you very lucky.'

'S'pose.'

'Right, but Pickles, well he doesn't have anyone to guide

him, apart from us. And I know it's different because he's a dog but he doesn't have any other dog friends. He probably misses his mum very much, he's just a baby.'

'I guess so. But what can I do about it?'

'You can be a big brother to him, like Aleksy, Henry and Toby all are. It's a very important, responsible role.'

'It is?'

'Of course, you've seen how much our human big brothers take care of the little ones, and it's a role that I think you are ready for.'

I noticed that Elvis and Nellie were listening and trying not to grin. We all knew the way to get George to agree to anything was flattery.

'In fact,' I continued, 'you would probably make the best big brother ever.'

No,' George said. Which surprised me.

'Why not?' I asked.

'He doesn't live with me so he can't be my brother.' He wouldn't meet my eyes.

'What about a cousin then?' Nellie suggested. 'I'm like an aunt to you, George, so how about you be a big cousin to Pickles.'

'That's a great idea, Nellie.' I nuzzled her in gratitude.

'But what do I have to do as a big cousin?' George asked.

'You can teach him things,' Elvis said.

'Yes,' Nellie added. 'You are a cat, and he's a dog, but there's still plenty you can show him.'

'You mean that I can teach him things that I can do?' George at least sounded interested now.

'That's right, George. You can also show him how to be

40

kind, how to be caring, all the important lessons that we taught you,' I added.

'And what about you? You can't be his dad because you're my dad,' he said, and I heard jealousy rearing up in his voice.

'If you're like a cousin to him then maybe I can be a bit like an uncle to him. Does that sound OK with you? Because you are my son, my number one and you always will be, understood?'

'Yes, you're right, we need to be nice to Pickles. He can be my friend, after all.' George hopped around, and even I was surprised by the sudden change in attitude.

'Oh George, that's so great, and you'll grow to love him, I'm sure you will.' I crossed my paws he would anyway.

'After all, I have a very big heart,' George said.

'You do,' Nellie agreed, in the motherly way of hers.

'The biggest,' Elvis added, he was a wise cat, when he felt like it, as he licked his paw.

'And I am proud of you every single day,' I added, as emotion overwhelmed me.

'A bit like how I was friends with Hana when she moved from Japan and was lonely, I can try to be the same with Pickles. But Hana's my best friend, so I won't like Pickles as much as I like her.'

'That's OK.' I sensed the need for baby steps.

'You're right, Dad. Pickles is a silly puppy, who doesn't know anything, right?'

'I'm not sure about the silly part but yes,' I agreed. Actually, he was silly, but I was trying to get George to bond with him, not tease him.

'So, I need to teach him everything I know,' George added.

'Exactly,' I agreed.

'I will do what you asked, and I will start tomorrow morning. I'm going to teach Pickles catting.'

'Eh?' Nellie said.

'It makes sense. Pickles is a dog, and everyone knows they're not as good as cats, so I will increase his chances by teaching him to be like me.'

Nellie, Elvis and I blinked at each other. It wasn't quite what I had in mind, but seeing as I had somehow led him to this place I couldn't argue. I didn't have a paw to stand on after all.

'It's more about teaching him things you know,' I reiterated.

'And I know how to be a cat. So that is what I will teach him. I'm going to teach Pickles how to be a cat, and I just can't wait to get started.'

Chapter Six

The education of Pickles would have to wait because we had headed next door to Sylvie's for a Japanese night. The night started out badly when Jonathan was late, because of his new job, which led to an angry hushed exchange at our house between him and Claire. I knew it was because he wanted to change out of his suit, but Claire said he didn't have time, and that he should have left work earlier. I could see both points, Jonathan was working hard, which he had warned us he would have to, but the reality wasn't as easy as the theory, it seemed.

Sylvie served up some wonderful Japanese food, including raw fish – sashimi – for me, Hana and George before the humans were seated. It was delicious. When Sylvie hosted Japanese night, as many of our families who could make it usually attended. Tonight Polly and Matt couldn't be there, and Tomasz was working, so it was just Claire and Jonathan, Franceska, her children, Aleksy and Tommy, along with Harold, Sylvie, Marcus and Connie. And us cats of course. Our children were being looked after by our babysitter, Rosie, who lived on our street and helped out for us all from time to time.

'Who's hungry?' Sylvie asked, ushering everyone to sit around their large dining table where the colourful food was laid out waiting for the humans. I wanted to bound over and get stuck in, but I had to show Hana and George manners, so I held back, although my mouth was literally watering from the taster I'd enjoyed beforehand. Harold made a huge fuss of George as usual as he slowly made his way over to the feast.

'Have you got any bread? Any English food?' Harold asked, once seated. He insisted on coming to Japanese night, but he refused to eat the food. Perhaps there was some hope of an extra portion?

'I'll get you some, Harold,' Connie offered. 'Would you like a sandwich?' she asked, sweetly.

'If you insist and a nice bit of ham wouldn't go amiss,' he mumbled.

'Anything for you, Harold,' Sylvie said. She was so calm and patient these days, which with Harold you had to be.

'Wine?' Marcus asked, filling up glasses with a warm smile.

'Yes please,' Tommy asked, and giggled. Out of the two boys he was the most likely to get into trouble.

'Tommy, you are far too young,' Franceska chastised, ruffling his hair in her maternal fashion.

'As are you, Connie, before you get any ideas,' Sylvie added but it was all in good humour. Tommy was nearly thirteen, and Connie and Aleksy almost fifteen, growing up so fast. When I first met Tommy, he was still in a pushchair. Goodness, that made me feel old.

'So how's the puppy settling in?' Marcus asked.

'Ah, he's gorgeous,' Claire said. 'So sweet and so much fun.'

'But not as gorgeous as our George,' Harold said, and I purred in agreement.

'I can't wait to meet him,' Connie added. Claire had organised a sort of 'welcome to the family' party for him at the weekend, which of course annoyed George. His whiskers had definitely been put out of joint.

'I know, I haven't even seen him yet,' Jonathan added. 'Working long hours means I barely see my own family let alone the new puppy.' He sounded sad, and I did worry about him. He and Claire said it would only be like this while he settled into his new job, and I just hoped it wouldn't take too long for things to change.

'But the weekend will be lovely, having us all together,' Claire reiterated. 'Harold, you're definitely coming, aren't you?'

'As long as we get some normal food,' he blustered.

'Luckily we don't get easily offended,' Marcus laughed. But we were all used to Harold's ways, and we loved him for it.

'Then after lunch, we can watch the footie together, Harold,' Jonathan said.

'Now, you're talking.' He grinned.

'Can we do anything?' Sylvie asked.

'No, all under control, just bring yourselves,' Claire beamed.

'And Tomasz has promised he will definitely be here,' Franceska said. Tomasz could work too hard at the restaurant as well, but he was much better lately now he had a full team of staff in place.

'I'll probably be the one to play most with the puppy,' Tommy said.

'How come?' his mum asked.

'Because I'm the odd one out now. Connie and Aleksy spend the whole time holding hands and making gooey noises, and the other children are still really young kids, so I am in the middle. I'll train the puppy, I might get him to do some tricks. Even teach him to dance.'

Good luck with that, I thought, as I headed over to experience our feast.

I sat back and cleaned myself up, hoping that a morsel might make its way in my direction. George and Hana were occupied, their little heads almost touching, and paws entwined. I was just glad they had each other.

'George told me all about the puppy,' Hana said, as I joined them. 'He sounds interesting,' she said carefully.

'Pickles, he's quite exhausting but quite sweet, Hana. I'm sure you'll meet him soon,' I said.

'I would like to meet him, I've never met a dog before, but I'm a little nervous,' she said. She'd lived a very sheltered life in Japan.

'Don't worry, Hana I will be right by your side when you do,' George said, puffing his chest out.

'Oh George, you are the best,' she replied.

'Then I'm excited to meet him,' she finished, with a grin. I smiled, because these two were like chalk and cheese. George, a bundle of energy who barely ever stood still and Hana, so calm, even the way she moved was sleek and graceful. George had all the grace of a dog. Oh goodness, now with Pickles in our lives, I really ought to stop thinking that way.

I left my boy happily playing with Hana, and I went back to see the humans. I jumped onto Aleksy's lap and let him fuss over me. He also gave me some of his leftovers, which I received gratefully.

'Does Alfie like the puppy?' Aleksy asked.

'You know Alfie, he's kind to everyone,' Claire said, echoing my thoughts.

'But you know, cats don't always like dogs,' Jonathan pointed out.

'Alfie and George seem to have taken to him, and he already adores them. He follows them around everywhere.'

'Alfie, you need to come to our house soon, Dustbin has been really busy, but he'd like to see you,' Tommy said. Franceska, Tomasz, Aleksy and Tommy lived a few streets away from Edgar Road, and I visited them often, I even stayed there sometimes, but I hadn't been over since before the holiday. With everything going on, I just hadn't had a minute. Dustbin worked for the restaurant, he kept the rodents at bay, and we were great friends. He was a feral cat with one of the biggest hearts I knew. He'd helped me get out of a few scrapes over the years, and I missed spending time with him. I wondered if it would be safe to leave George and Pickles alone the following day. It might give George a sense of responsibility and also allow him and Pickles to bond a bit. That way we all win, George would get to be a big brother, or cousin rather, and I got time off. Perfect, it was another good plan.

'Tomorrow we have careers day,' Aleksy said.

'What's that?' Jonathan asked.

'It's a day of learning about different jobs that we might want to do, so we can begin to think about it,' Connie explained.

'God, you are so young, I had no idea what I wanted to do until about ten years ago,' Marcus said.

'I'm not sure I've decided yet,' Jonathan joked.

'Not helpful,' Claire chastised.

'What do you do?' Tommy asked Marcus.

'I had my own business, but I sold it, so now I work for a business advisory company, where we help companies find ways to grow. I actually quite like it,' Marcus explained. Tommy made a face.

'And I work in investments in the City,' Jonathan added.

'I'm going to be a fireman,' Tommy announced. 'I like to save people, and I like fires.' No one really wanted to comment on that, and stayed quiet.

'I think I'd like to work in restaurants,' Aleksy said.

'Ah, you just want to suck up to mum and dad,' Tommy shot.

'No I do not, I think the business side would be interesting. I like hospitality, and I like the fact that we make people happy with our food.'

'Ah, *kochanie*, we would love for you to work with us one day, but it has to be what you want to do.' *Kochanie* was a Polish term of affection, Franceska used it a lot.

'What about you, Connie?'

'I'd like to be a solicitor, I think. Once I'm qualified, I can travel if I want to, or stay here.'

'Her father's a solicitor,' Sylvie said; her voice filled with sadness and her eyes clouded over. It was a 'Sylvie moment', and it could go either way.

'Maybe it's in the blood then,' Marcus quickly cut in, diffusing the situation. He was good at that. She was still bitter about her ex-husband and rightfully so, he went off with a younger woman and they recently had a baby. Connie's father still lived in Japan, which was very hard for her, as she only got to speak to him on Skype occasionally. Marcus, though, was a top bloke. He knew how to handle the situation, and I was grateful that Sylvie had welcomed him into their lives.

'It might be in my blood, I think it is,' Connie finished. 'Now I have to work hard and get the grades I need to study law at a good university.'

'Right, let's help with the clearing up,' Franceska suggested and as chairs began scraping along the floor, and plates clanked together, all felt right once again.

George and I sat on the back doorstep of our house and watched the stars.

'So tomorrow I'm in charge of the dog?' George said, puffing his chest out importantly.

'You and Pickles can spend some time alone, so you can share your wisdom with him,' I said. 'Remember, the most important thing, you need to be kind to Pickles.'

'I will be, but does Pickles have to do everything I say?'

'I think that sounds a bit more like you're going to boss him around, rather than teach him.'

'OK, but he's the youngest. If he does something wrong, I can tell him to stop? I'm the boss because I'm the oldest.'

'You absolutely can do that, as long as you tell him nicely.'

'So I am in charge then.'

There was no point in arguing further. We enjoyed the night air for a bit longer, before we headed inside. I tucked George in where he slept on the end of Toby's bed on his own blanket. It was so sweet, the bond they shared. At times like this, as I saw my family and my friends, I counted my blessings. Tomorrow I would see my other friend, which would make me very happy indeed. I just hoped and prayed that George and Pickles would be alright together. And that the house was still standing when I got home.

Chapter
Seven

Chapter
Seven

The following morning, I took my time strolling to Franceska and Tomasz' place. Autumn was in the air, and leaves were turning brown on the trees, ready to shed. It was one of my favourite times because I loved playing with leaves. It was a sunny but chilly day, and I intended to enjoy the time alone. Since becoming a parent, I had come to value alone time. Now that George was older and went off on his own, I veered from worrying about him to enjoying a bit of peace. However, since being joined by Pickles, I was reminded of when George was a tiny kitten, and I had barely any time to myself. As I enjoyed my walk, I passed a lot of legs on the pavement, people rushing around, busily, no one seemed as chilled as I was. I dodged some pushchair wheels and nearly got stepped on a couple of times, but I was an expert in dodging humans. I even saw a couple of dogs, on leads, and I tried to smile at them, but they didn't seem to be that keen to smile back. Maybe my new relationship with the dog world would take time.

When I arrived, I scooted around the back of the restaurant through the alley I knew well, and headed to the dustbin area where I knew I would find my friend, Dustbin. He was aptly named. Even if he was a bit scruffy looking, and could be a little fragrant at times, I adored him. As did George.

'Dustbin,' I said, and then stopped. Next to him was a scruffy-looking female cat, who I had never seen before.

'Ah Alfie,' he greeted me. 'What a nice surprise.'

'Who is this?' I asked as the cat, who on closer inspection was a ginger cat with very green eyes, gave me the once-over.

'This is Ally, she lives in the next alley. We met when she strayed into my yard while you were away, and then she offered to help with the rodents, so we've been hanging out ever since.'

If cats could blush, I am pretty sure that Dustbin might have done so. In fact, I swear his whiskers turned a bit pink. Dustbin, although happy to be friends, was more of a loner cat so this was definitely a turn up for the paws. I was proud of him, and I was pleased for him if it was what I thought it was anyway.

'Nice to meet you,' Ally said. She looked a little shy suddenly, which for a big feral cat wasn't that usual.

'You too,' I replied, as we looked at each other. 'So you're new around here?'

'Not really. I live a few roads away, but then I was exploring one day and came across this place, met Dustbin, and we just got talking.'

'So do you have a family or do you live outside like Dustbin?'

'I'm a street cat,' Ally explained. 'I've never lived with a family myself. Dustbin told me so much about you and I thought that you sound nice and I've met the family who lives here, so I am very happy to meet you.'

'Good to meet you too,' I said.

'Right, Alfie, I've got things to do. I'll leave you two to it. See you later, Dustbin.'

'See you later, Ally,' Dustbin said, not quite meeting her eyes.

'Bye,' I said as she swished her tail as she strutted away. 'Well, well well,' I teased when Dustbin and I were alone.

'Stop it, Alfie, I mean I know you always told me how

nice female company was, but I'm a loner cat as you know. Then I met Ally and well, I can't explain it, I just like hanging out with her.'

'That is so great, and there's nothing wrong with it. You like spending time with me as well,' I pointed out.

'Yeah but it's different with Ally, I can't explain it, and I'm probably far too old to be feeling like this, but I look forward to spending all my time with her, and I never want to be apart from her. Even now I kind of miss her.' He sounded so young and unsure as he explained this.

'Sorry, Dustbin, but you're in love, it's clear to see.' I did a little hop, I loved to see my friends happy.

'Don't know about that, but she's alright,' he replied gruffly. I could see through his facade, he was different, had a bit more of a spring in his step, and he definitely seemed happier.

'Right, well then, why don't you and I find a nice sunny spot to chill out in, and you can tell me all about alright Ally.'

'She's a very good mouser,' he said, sounding impressed and then he continued to talk about her.

It was both wonderful and slightly weird to see Dustbin this way. Only because he had never been one for other cats or people. Although he had grown fond of George and me, it was more because I didn't give him much choice in the matter. When we first met he wasn't that keen on being friends really. So to see him talking about Ally with his eyes lighting up and his voice almost bashful, it was definitely unexpected. Of course, I was happy for him. I'd been in love twice after all, so although it hurt when it was over, it was wonderful while I had it. Claire always went on about some bloke who said 'it was better to have loved and lost than never to have loved at all,' or something like that, and I totally agreed with that. Because love and loss go hand in hand, but they also both mean you are alive, your heart still beating. Listen to me; Dustbin had made me get all nostalgic and gooey. What was the world coming to?

'If you ever need any advice about women, you know where to come,' I offered as I stretched my paws out and got ready to leave. I needed to get back and make sure that Pickles and George were alright. Although part of me didn't want to go there at all, terrified of what I might find.

'Thanks, Alfie, but you know, it'll be, you know, fine. I mean it's nothing to worry about.' He was still feigning nonchalance, but I saw how he really felt. We said our good-byes, and I smiled all the way home.

The smile disappeared from my face as soon as I got through the cat flap. Claire was chasing Pickles. Arms outstretched she was running around after him but every time she got close he seemed to dodge her. Her face was getting redder and redder.

'Pickles, drop, bad puppy,' she said. George was sitting by idly licking his paws. What had he done? When Claire caught Pickles, she picked him up and took one of Jonathan's favourite slippers – Italian and expensive – out of his mouth. Oh no, Jonathan would be furious.

'Oh thank goodness you're back, Alfie,' Claire said. She looked a little frazzled. 'These two have been running me ragged. Firstly, Pickles managed to get stuck under the sofa, and I have no idea how that happened, then he chewed a chair leg. All I did was visit Harold to take him his lunch and came back to find that George and Pickles were nowhere to be seen. I panicked and then found them in the garden, they'd got through the cat flap. Then finally he stole Jonathan's favourite slipper, and he's going to be so cross. How can a puppy be so much work? I'm going to collect the children. Please make sure that nothing happens when I'm gone.' She barely took a breath before she left the house and stalked off.

'Who wants to tell me what's going on?' I asked when alone with George and Pickles.

'It was so much fun,' Pickles said.

'I was teaching him what I knew,' George said. 'Just like you said. So, I showed him the warm spot under the sofa, how was I supposed to know he wouldn't be able to get out? And I can't take responsibility for the chair leg, I did tell him that cats don't chew things, but he's not that quick to learn. He also licks everything which I think is weird.'

'And the garden?'

'I needed to go out, you know, for obvious reasons and he followed me through the cat flap. So you see, none of this is really my fault.'

The joys of parenting.

'Right, listen up, both of you,' I started in my sternest voice. 'Pickles, George is right, we don't chew things, so please can you try to keep your chewing to your toys.' I walked over to his nice soft bed, full of toys that he could chew.

'OK.' he said, but as George said, he was young and I wasn't sure if he understood or if I would have to tell him lots more times.

'Secondly, if George goes out, then I don't see why you can't go with him as long as you both promise to stay in the garden.'

'I promise I won't let him leave the garden,' George said.

'Besides I need to learn to climb the tree,' Pickles said,

'Seriously?' I turned to George, who tried not to smile. I swished my tail. George was definitely having a bit of fun with Pickles. Someday soon, Pickles would learn for himself that he can't climb trees, I was pretty sure he couldn't anyway.

'So, on the whole, did I do good, Dad?' George asked.

'Not bad for your first day,' I conceded, but I wasn't entirely convinced. Claire clearly wasn't anyway, but I needed to encourage George and Pickles' relationship in whatever way I could.

'And me, was I good?' Pickles asked. I chose to pretend that I hadn't heard. It was easier.

Thankfully before any more trouble could occur, the door opened, and Claire and the four children rushed in. They all headed for the kitchen and made a fuss of all of us, which was nice for George, before demanding snacks.

'We're going to put Pickles on the lead and take him to the park,' Summer announced bossily. She was wearing her school uniform, her fair hair in a ponytail was bobbing behind her.

'I'm so going to hold the lead,' Henry said. He was the biggest of our younger children, very tall for his age, and he looked a little like his father with his light brown hair and nose sprinkled with freckles.

'But I want to,' Martha asked. Martha was usually the most laid-back of the children, apart from when it came to Pickles it seemed. She was such a pretty child with dark hair and big dark eyes. Polly, her mum, used to be a model and she often said that Martha took after her.

'And me,' Summer shouted.

'But what about me?' Toby said. Toby was the same age as Henry but was smaller. He had sandy blond hair and serious blue eyes. He was so gentle which with bossy Summer as a sister was a very good thing.

'Listen.' Claire had her best parenting voice on. 'We will all take turns looking after Pickles. I will have to take him across the roads because I'm the grown-up, and the rest of the time you will have equal time holding the lead, I'll use the stopwatch.'

None of them argued with that. If only Pickles and George were so easy to control.

I was tired by the time everyone had left for the park. I lay down on the sofa, and George joined me. We snuggled up together, which was lovely, and rare these days. George was usually too busy or pleaded to be too old for a cuddle with his old dad. He told me all about his day with Pickles.

'He's quite funny really, but then so naughty, and also a bit too easy to tease, so I'm sorry, but when I told him to stop chewing, he really didn't listen. And he tried to eat my food, which he doesn't even like. When I pointed out that you already told him it was cat food, he claimed he forgot. I think it might be harder than I first thought for him to be like me.'

'Keep trying,' I said, deciding not to tell him that I didn't necessarily want Pickles to be like George, but to humour him for now. 'And you'll never guess what I found out today.'

'What?' George's ears pricked up, he loved gossip.

'Dustbin has got a girlfriend,' I said.

'No way! Oh my goodness, Dustbin who said love was soppy and he didn't have time for all that, as he had too many mice to catch?'

'Exactly. But I think he's met a kindred spirit. Ally, from a nearby street actually, and she sees off the rodents with him.'

'She sounds like the perfect match for him.'

I nodded, and purred, my boy was pretty perceptive. Now, if only he could teach Pickles that quality, we'd all be alright.

'I like that Dustbin is happy. Can we visit him soon, and maybe I'll get to meet Ally from the alley too.'

'Of course, I'll take you one day soon, when we don't have to puppy-sit. I wonder if his relationship with Ally the same as yours and Hana's.' I was trying to dig, of course, I was.

'I am getting to like Pickles a little bit. Especially watching him try to climb trees, it was so funny, he kept trying to grip his front claws, but they slid down, and he ended up on his bottom. The best thing was that he kept trying, which I suppose either shows great character or extreme stupidity, I'm not sure which.' So he wasn't giving me anything, as usual.

'Let's go for great character, it's nicer,' I replied, although I wasn't sure that was the right answer either.

'And then when Claire found us in the garden, she was a bit cross, so she took him inside, and he fell asleep straight away, you should have heard how loudly he snores. He sounds like a train.'

'But you like him?' I asked.

'Yes, I like him. A bit anyway.'

This was progress. We snuggled up together, and both fell asleep.

Chapter
Eight

'Oh for goodness' sake, George, can you stop trying to trip me up,' Claire snapped, as George followed her around, hanging around her legs too closely and hoping to get some scraps of food she was carrying. But Claire, preparing for the family get-together was stressed enough, without George adding to it.

'George,' I hissed. Trying to get him to come over. He bounded over to me.

'What?' he asked, looking at me innocently.

'You know better than to annoy Claire when she's stressed.'

'But the food smells so good.'

'And if we keep out of her way, we'll get something nice, but for now, we need to let her get on with it.'

'Claire, how much food do we really need?' Jonathan asked, coming into the kitchen.

'I don't want anyone to go hungry,' Claire replied.

'You know it's a good job I got a promotion; otherwise there's no way we could afford all this,' Jonathan moaned.

'Oh shut up and go and get the drinks ready. Oh, and can you give the cats some food, to keep them out of my way.'

'Meow!' I objected, I wasn't in her way, it was all George. But I grinned at George, we were getting food, his annoying ways had worked in both our favour.

Family days were utterly precious, and my heart was full as the doorbell kept going, heralding the arrival of the people we loved.

Polly, Matt, the children and guest of honour Pickles arrived first. The children all crowded round Pickles, which I could tell annoyed George, although he had played with Summer and Toby that morning. Before I had much time to be fussed over by Matt, the door went again and in came, Tomasz, Franceska, Aleksy and Tommy. They made a huge fuss of George and me, which placated George. Tomasz picked Georgia up and cuddled him, Aleksy did the same to me. Franceska gave us both a stroke and Tommy took George out of Tomasz's arms and ticked his head the way he loved. Before they even got past the hallway, the door went again. Sylvie and Connie came in, Connie make a beeline for Aleksy and Sylvie raising her eyebrows, but not objecting as they went off to the living room hand in hand.

'Marcus has just gone to get Harold, so they'll be here any minute. But I have to warn you, Harold said he didn't sleep so well, so he's a little moody today.'

'Don't worry, I'm sure George will cheer him up.' George preened at that. He was the only one who could cheer Harold up after all, and I was so glad for anything that made him feel good about himself.

'Watch what we taught Pickles,' Henry said, to all of us. We watched. 'Right, sit,' Henry commanded. Pickles wagged his tail but didn't sit. 'SIT,' Henry shouted. Pickles didn't move,

'You're not doing it right, do it like this,' Martha said. 'Pickles, sit down,' she commanded in her sweet voice, with a smile. Pickles barked.

'I can do it,' Toby said. 'Pickles sit,' he shouted. Pickles walked to the other side of the hall.

'PICKLES, SIT RIGHT NOW!' Summer shrieked. Pickles sat down, but then so did we all.

'Well Summer wins the training prize I guess,' Polly said.

'No, she's just the scariest,' Claire said. 'Summer, the secret to good puppy training is not to shout at him, he's a baby, and you could scare him.' She'd certainly scared me after all. Just as all hell threatened to break loose as Summer didn't take criticism well, we were once again saved by the doorbell, and Marcus and Harold appeared. George, taking no chances, leapt into Harold's arms, taking him by surprise.

'Come in, and let's get this party started,' Claire said excitedly as everyone filed to different rooms in the house in a way which showed how used to being here everyone was. Like a proper family.

'I'm happy to be here but to be honest, it's getting colder than I like,' Harold blustered. He loved to have something to complain about. It was September, and it wasn't as hot as summer but it was hardly cold yet.

'I can put the heating on for you,' Claire offered, giving Harold a hug.

'No, I can't be doing with that central heating, it kills people,' Harold said.

Really? Did it?

'I don't think it does, Dad,' Marcus said, steering him to a chair. George was still attached to him. Those two, I thought, fondly.

'Mark my words, in a few years' time everyone will be talking about it. It'll come out that it's causing that global warming and the ozone layer and the lack of polar bears.'

George licked Harold's face, he thought he was the cleverest man in the world.

I did sometimes wonder where Harold got his complaints from, and by the looks on the faces of my humans, they did too. Thankfully they all loved him very much.

I was in heaven as I moved from room to room to check on my loved ones. The women were in the kitchen, drinking wine, eating and chatting. The men were all in the living room, with drinks, plates of food and George who hadn't left Harold's side sitting together on the chair he was settled in. I had a suspicion they were sharing food, but I was too happy to tell him off. As long as he was having a good time, I would have to accept it. The children, along with Pickles, were upstairs joined by Tommy, who protested he was too old to hang out with the younger ones but actually secretly enjoyed making up games for them to play. What he'd done was to set up an obstacle course for Pickles on the upstairs landing. There was a toy horse jump, a tunnel that Summer used to love when she was little, a hoop which one of them had to hold for him to jump through and a stool for him to climb on and off. Pickles seemed very confused by this and kept getting it wrong.

'No, Pickles, you don't sit down in the tunnel,' Summer who was the bossiest of all the children chided. Even her words didn't work this time. The problem was that Polly had taught them that if they wanted Pickles to do something, they had to offer a treat as a reward, but they were giving him treats before he did anything. All the treats had gone, and Pickles was none the wiser in how to do an assault course.

'I know,' Tommy said. 'I'll go and get George, he can show Pickles how it's done.'

I raised my whiskers, George, hopefully, would be pleased to be given such a role. I waited until Tommy came back upstairs, George wriggling in his arms. He didn't seem that happy, actually.

'Right, George, please can you show Pickles how to do an obstacle course,' Tommy begged. George came to where I was and sat with his back to the children. Oh dear.

'What's wrong?' I whispered.

'They ignore me, and now they want me to show the dumb puppy how to do something so basic,' he hissed back.

'George, they love you, they pretty much ignored me too, but Pickles is new to them. Perhaps show them how fantastic you are and it might help Pickles too,' I coaxed, gently.

'I am fantastic, aren't I?'

'You are, son.'

'Meow,' George said loudly and he went to join the children. As they cheered him, I saw him preen, and I was happy how easy it was for us all to be friends, or almost friends in any case.

Connie and Aleksy sat on the stairs holding hands and whispering to each other, but the important thing is that they didn't sneak off into one of the bedrooms, so I didn't have to worry too much. I jumped onto Aleksy's lap.

'Hey, Alfie,' Aleksy gave me a nice head scratch.

'I tried to bring Hana, but she didn't want to come, I think she just wanted some peace and quiet,' Connie said. I didn't blame her for staying away, this was not for the faint-hearted, although she normally came with us, she didn't always. Suddenly Pickles knocked into George, and sent him flying, with caused George to yowl and land on his tail. Then George, showing his balance, fell off the stool and landed on Pickles, who cried out, but seemed unhurt, and the children all shrieked with laughter. George really did seem to be taking Pickles under his wing and he tried to show him calmly exactly how an obstacle course was done.

'Wow, Pickles actually does follow George,' Toby said. 'He's almost doing it right now!'

George basked in all the praise.

'Right, children, can you come and eat please.' Claire's voice floated up the stairs. Everyone carried on doing what they were doing. 'NOW,' she shouted, and we all traipsed downstairs, the children a little reluctantly, I was far keener.

George and I had a bowl of fat pilchards awaiting us, and Pickles tried to muscle in.

'Not for you,' Matt said, scooping him up, thankfully. I was a very tolerant cat, but no one came between me and my pilchards. Pickles let out a cry. 'No, Pickles, you need to eat only puppy food, mate, I'm afraid. You don't want to get fat do you?'

Pickles looked as if he would very much like to get fat.

After eating, the children went out into the garden, Pickles was fast asleep in his bed, and George and I were satisfyingly full after our lovely meal. Harold was asleep in the living room, snoring contentedly. I felt my heart swell with love for all my friends and I wished it could always be like this.

Chapter Nine

I went through my mental checklist alone in the garden before Pickles would inevitably break through the cat flap again. It was October already, time was passing, and winter was creeping ever closer. I did prefer the warm weather, not least because I had an old leg injury, which flared up more in the winter. Anyway, I wasn't going to dwell on that. I was going to make the best of things, which is what this cat always did.

My chaperoning skills were going to be essential today because George hadn't been able to visit Hana for a couple of days. Knowing how happy they made each other, I knew he needed to do that. After Claire dropped the children at school, she'd be home most of today, so it wasn't as if I would be in sole charge of Pickles, thankfully.

Marcus took Harold to somewhere called a 'Senior Centre', a place where he could socialise with other old people, most of whom he claimed not to like, so I really had no idea why he went. But with a day to herself, Claire would clean the house, do the laundry, tidy all the children's rooms, and change all the bedding – it was quite exhausting to watch. When she'd finished that she would then sit down with a well-deserved cup of coffee and her book – and hopefully me, before going to pick the children up from school. It wasn't easy being a housewife, which I believe is her official job title. It was hard to see how anyone could have an outside job, and look after a house and children once you'd seen Claire in action.

Claire used to love working, she'd had a good job in marketing, but after she had Summer, she lost a bit of her ambition. Then when Toby came to live with us, she felt the children were her priority. It turned out she loved being a mum more than anything, and she was lucky, with Jonathan's job and the fact she was very sensible with money, she was able to devote herself to doing what she loved. Also, I was unsure how we would cope if Claire and Jonathan both worked as we all needed a lot of taking care of. Not to mention what would happen to Pickles after all. I like to think it was seeing me taking care of those I cared about that made Claire realise it was what she wanted to do. And we were both quite good at it.

Back to my checklist. All my humans were doing well at the moment, I thought, as I ran through them one by one. The children were happy and not arguing with each other, and of course, having Pickles had perked them up the way George had when he first came to live with us. Aleksy and Connie were happy and perhaps the most sensible teenagers the world had ever seen. And the adults were not causing me problems for once. We were all happy and harmonious on Edgar Road, including my extended families in the neighbourhood of course. Even Pickles.

Then there were the cats. Luckily my lovely friends were all fine; having lost Tiger I did fret about the other cats a bit, but they all seemed in good health. Dustbin's new girlfriend was definitely an interesting turn up for the books. George was coping; even though he still missed Tiger, but we were dealing with that. It would take a lot of time to heal. It became more important to me to understand what was actually going on with Hana and him. It wasn't just out of noisiness, but concern. Or that's my story, and I am sticking to it.

Life was calm, and I just crossed my paws that the turmoil of last year was long behind us. Not that having Pickles was particularly calm, but you know what I mean.

The cat flap bashed, and George sprang through it, followed at a more leisurely pace by Pickles.

'Hello, Alfie,' he said, as he stood on the grass then he bent down to lick it. He was actually very cute, even his wrinkly face seemed adorable to me now.

'Pickles, how are you?' I asked.

'I am very well. I was a bit sick this morning, but Polly said it was because I wasn't supposed to eat the children's breakfast – Henry fed me some off his plate, so he's in a bit of trouble but how am I to know?'

'It's hard, I agree. Pickles, the general rule of thumb is that if it's in your food bowl, then it's yours. If it's not, then it isn't,' I explained.

'No, that seems far too hard to remember.' His wrinkled face wrinkled even more. 'I think I'll just have to take my chances.'

'See what I mean?' George hissed. 'Pickles, show my dad how you climb trees.'

'Yes, yes, I will.' We watched as Pickles approached a tree in the garden, and started trying to climb its trunk. It was fruitless, his front legs slid off the bark as soon as he moved them. Then he decided he'd try to jump, but he couldn't jump very high yet, and landed with a bump. Yet again I had to intervene.

'Maybe tree climbing isn't going to be your thing. After all, I'm not keen either,' I said. George was studying his paws intently.

'But if I can't climb a tree then I'll never be a cat.'

'Pickles, you're a puppy who will grow up to be a dog, not a cat,' I said gently.

'But cats are best, George said so, so if I do everything he teaches me, I can grow up to be a cat.' Pickles turned to look at me, his eyes full of hope. What on earth could I say? I turned to look at George.

'I really need to go and see Hana,' he said as he ran off.

'How about we go inside, and I'll teach you how to have a lovely rest,' I suggested.

'Do cats do that?' he asked.

'Of course, it's one of the things we do best.' With no idea what we were getting into with Pickles, I ushered him back through the cat flap and into the house. Thankfully, our sofa was low enough for Pickles to jump on, so I led him there, jumped up and gestured for him to do the same. He wriggled around a bit on the sofa cushion, his little paws padding up and down. Then he chose a spot and licked a cushion before sitting on it. I didn't really understand dog behaviour, but then I had no experience. Give me a human or a cat any day.

'So, lie down, and then we can both close our eyes and have a rest. That's very good cat behaviour.' I felt guilty for using George's naughty plan, but then I was quite tired, I'd already done quite a lot of thinking today.

'OK.' He lay down, resting his head on his paws and before long he was snoring quite loudly. When I was sure he was asleep, I thought I could steal a few minutes away.

I left through the cat flap, went as fast as I could next door and round to the back of Sylvie's house. At the back were patio doors. I couldn't go in, because there was no way George could know I was there, he would kill me. But it wasn't actually spying, I was only doing what a good parent would do.

I positioned myself in a bush near the doors, and I craned my neck and glanced through. Hana was lying on the floor in a sunny spot, and George was sitting next to her. I could see they were chatting, but of course, I couldn't hear or see what they were talking about.

This brought back memories. When my first girlfriend Snowball moved in here I used to spend hours by the back door trying to get her attention. She accused me of stalking her once. But in the end, I did get her attention. OK, so it might have involved a near death experience, the fire brigade and a ruined flowerbed but that's another story.

I tried to move a little closer, trying to balance on the bush to lift me a bit. However, my paw slipped, and I ended up falling through the middle, onto some soft soil. I got up, brushed my fur off, and feeling a little silly I snuck another look. Although George and Hana definitely seemed close, it was still inconclusive. I went home, none the wiser.

I got home, thankfully before Pickles woke up. I snuggled next to him, so he would wake and think I'd been there all along. I was so tired I almost fell asleep when a wet nose touched my cheek. I stretched, wishing that I had another forty winks.

'That was a nice rest, but now I want to play,' Pickles said.

'What do you want to play?' I asked. This was bringing

back memories, memories of George as a tiny kitten, always wanting to do something.

'I don't know, the only games I know are the ones George taught me.' He looked thoughtful.

'Did he teach you to play hide and seek?' I asked.

'No, can we play that?' He started wagging his tail and wiggling his bottom simultaneously.

'Yes, what happens is that I count to a certain number—'

'What's count?'

'Don't worry, we'll teach you one day. Anyway,' I continued, 'I count and you hide somewhere, and then I come and find you.'

'Wowee that sounds like fun.' Pickles was so excited he forgot where he was and fell off the sofa, landing on his back.

'Are you alright?' I asked; puppy-sitting was hard work.

'Yes, fine.' He bounced up. 'Right I'm going to be the best hider ever.'

I lay down and pretended to count for as long as I thought I could get away with. George had always loved hide and seek, and it was my favourite game because it gave me a few moments of peace while I counted. Top parenting tip for you.

Finally, I had to go and find Pickles. I padded through the hall and then into the kitchen. He was sat on the floor with his head in a cereal box. Although I could see his body, it wasn't a bad hiding place, actually.

'Found you,' I said, approaching.

'Hmmph.' A vague sound came from the box.

'You can take the box off now, I've found you,' I said, edging closer to try to hear him.

'I'm stuck,' he replied, his voice still muffled. The next thing I knew he was running round in circles, cereal crumbs falling onto his fur and the floor before he bumped into a cupboard door. 'Ow,' he cried.

I sighed. I wasn't sure what to do. I was a cat, after all, and I had paws, which meant I wasn't sure how I could get the box off.

'Calm down, Pickles. Right, lie down, and I'll see if I can grab the box,' I commanded. He lay down, still wiggling. He did look funny. I tried to grip the box with my paws but they just slid off. Pickles was really quite stuck. I began to panic. I was the worst puppy-sitter ever. George had got into quite a few scrapes as a kitten: stuck in bags, boxes, and various cupboards, but I could deal with cat scrapes. Puppy scrapes were a whole different ball game.

'I can't live in this box forever,' Pickles said, sadly, and I redoubled my efforts, but it really wasn't budging. Thankfully I heard the door open and in walked Claire. I sat up and looked at her, my eyes full of guilt.

'What on earth?' Claire pulled the box off Pickles and picked him up. He was covered in cereal.

'Meow,' I said, it wasn't my fault.

'Oh goodness, I better clean this mess up. I guess puppies can be hard to look after,' Claire said, gently, holding Pickles in one arm and petting me with the other, to show she wasn't angry.

'Meow,' I agreed, relieved.

'Right, well, Pickles, stay in there, while I get this cleared up.' She brushed the cereal from his fur and set him down in his bed. I went over to him.

'Not the best hiding place after all, then, Pickles,' I said.

'Oh, I wasn't hiding. I was going to find somewhere to hide then I spotted the cereal box on the floor.' Why was it on the floor? I wondered. One of the children I guessed.

'So, what were you doing?'

'I wanted to have a snack, so I got the box on its side and then I went in to get my snack, and I somehow got stuck.'

Of course he did.

'But it was quite delicious,' he finished. 'But next time I'll have to find an easier way to get it.'

Claire took Pickles with her while she cleaned the house, saying it was the only way she could keep him out of trouble. I wasn't sorry, as I went out and bumped into George who was coming from Hana's house.

'Hi, son,' I said, happy to see him. 'What have you been up to?' As if I didn't know.

'Just talking to Hana. What about you?'

I told him about Pickles and the cereal.

'When I was young I didn't do stuff like that,' George tutted.

'Well, you nearly drowned, got stuck in lots of cupboards, were catnapped, and that's just for starters,' I pointed out, although technically the catnapping was my fault.

I had come up with a plan to solve a little scrape my human owner was in by pretending to lose George, and hiding him in Tiger's shed. But he ended up being catnapped, and it was the worst time of my entire life until I found him. The plan did work eventually, it did bring us all together, but I learned a big lesson and would never put my kitten in the slightest risk ever again.

'OK, fair enough, but now I'm a big cat, things have changed,' he said. 'Shall we go for a walk?'

'Yes, come on, then.' We started off towards the end of the street.

'You know about me being a big cat,' George said as we strolled.

'Yes?' I asked. Clearly, he wanted to talk to me about something.

'What is my job?'

'What do you mean your job?' I asked.

'My job, you know Hana was telling me how Connie and Aleksy were talking all the time about what they were going to do when they were grown-ups. Well, I'm pretty much a grown-up now, and I don't have a job.'

'We're cats, George, I don't have a job either.'

'But you do, I mean you don't have an office like Jonathan, but like Claire, you take care of all of us, that's your job the way it is hers, so what's mine?'

'Being a big cousin to Pickles is a job of sorts then,' I explained.

'Yeah, maybe it's a bit of a job, but it's not my cat calling. I need to find my purpose in life.'

'Your purpose in life?'

'You take care of people and Dustbin has a job taking care of the rodents, so I need to find my life purpose.' He was getting frustrated.

'I guess you have a point.' I wasn't sure that George needed a job, after all, I had kind of stumbled into my role. And I had no training for it, not to mention that the pay was terrible apart from the odd pilchard. But he sounded so serious about this, I had to give him my support.

'Yes, I might be a cat, but I'm not an ordinary cat, so therefore I need to find my purpose. What I am supposed to do to make the world a better place.'

'Wow, well when you put it like that, George, I guess, like me, your vocation will be to do the same as me.'

'I thought that but I need to find my own path in life, I can't just jump onto yours.'

'George, what on earth are you talking about?' I was bewildered.

'It's what Aleksy said. He is going to get a job working in a different restaurant and learn the hard way before joining the family business because otherwise, it will be too easy for him. Nepotism it's called. Hana told me, she's very clever. So I need to find my own job rather than take the easy route by following you.'

'George, you are a very clever cat, although you'll always be my kitten, so you can do whatever it is you put your mind to, but if you want any advice, you know where I am.' I crossed my paws that he would give me a bit of time before asking for my advice because I had no idea what to tell him. I was still trying to get my head around the concept of nepotism, which I'd never even heard of.

'Thanks, Dad, but as Aleksy told Connie and Hana, sometimes when you are growing up, you need to do things yourself for yourself. It's how you build character. So that's what I am going to do. I am going to make you proud of me.'

I couldn't argue with that.

'I'm so proud of you already, George,' I said, feeling emotional. My boy was growing up so fast, like Aleksy, who was also my boy and all of the children. I could see why Polly was so keen to get Pickles, keeping a baby in the family. Although after this morning I was pretty sure there had to be easier ways.

'I am going to be an amazing career cat, just as soon as I figure out what I am going to do with my life,' he announced, and I couldn't reply because I felt both choked up with pride and also a little amused. There weren't exactly a million jobs for cats, after all. But then if anyone could find something to do, it was George. I would help him in any way I could because that was what a parent did. And that was a job in itself, after all.

Chapter
Ten

Polly had a few days off work, so we didn't get to see Pickles as much as before, although he did pop in quite a lot so Polly could drink coffee and chat with Claire. But with the humans around, he wasn't able to get into too much trouble, because they stopped him the minute he started. George and I could only sit and watch Pickles well and truly under control. Or as under control as he could be.

'I'm thinking of sending Pickles to puppy training,' Polly said as she had coffee with Claire.

'But he's not that bad,' Claire said. 'And he's still so little.'

'He doesn't do what he's told,' Polly pointed out. Ever, I added.

'No, but he's housetrained which is the main thing, and he's still a baby. Besides, you're so busy that I might end up having to take him and I'm not sure I fancy it!' Claire pointed out. 'I can barely train my own family.' They both laughed. I narrowed my eyes, I was very well trained thank you very much, although Claire couldn't take the credit for that. In fact, it was me who trained my humans rather than vice versa.

'No, I've found a weekend class, and I think Matt can take him. After all, Matt was the one who pushed for him to come and live with us.'

'I'm not sure Matt is the best person to train him, Pol,' Claire said. I agreed. Matt was lovely but so soft, no one did what they were told when he was in charge.

'It might be good for both of them then. I thought I might get him to take Henry and Martha, they can have bonding time as well.'

'Actually, that's not a bad idea, it could be their thing. Jonathan is so busy at the moment, I'm worried the kids aren't getting enough time with him. So this Saturday we're going to have a fun day out in London together. I know Jonathan's not keen, he's so tired, but I've told him if he does Saturday with us then we'll have a pyjama and film day on Sunday.'

'So, he's still working ridiculously hard?'

'I really have to bite my tongue and not nag him. I mean we both discussed the fact that the job was going to change things before he took the promotion, but I guess the theory and the practice are two different things. I miss him, that's it really, I miss spending time with him.'

'But in the long run, it'll be worth it?' Polly asked.

'It's not just the money, I mean that's really good, and it means I can be there for the kids, but we also need to try to figure out how we can do this without ruining our family.'

'And you will figure it out. Now Matt and I are both working we have to make time for us, so that's the first thing. You two need time as a couple, and you are always looking after my children, so perhaps we can reciprocate? You just need to be organised and, Claire, that is your strong point after all.' Polly leant over and grabbed Claire's hand and gave it a squeeze.

'You know you're right. I think instead of worrying I should see what we can do. If Jonathan and I have a night out that would be a start.'

I felt my heart sink a little, I thought everything was alright in our world, and to be honest, Claire was handling it well, but it did set off a little warning bell in my mind. I would have to keep an eye on this.

'Right, well Matt and I can have the kids, perhaps they can have a sleepover, so you guys can have the night to yourself.'

'Now you're talking.' Claire smiled as did I. With friends like ours, nothing seemed to be insurmountable. 'Right, I'm going to see Harold, fancy a walk down with me?'

'Sure, but I won't stop after saying hello, as I have to walk Pickles.'

They set off with Pickles on the lead and George decided that he wanted to go after them.

'That's fine, are you worried about Pickles?' I asked.

'Someone needs to keep an eye on him, and Harold prefers cats to dogs so I should be there to make it easier for him,' he said, sounding very responsible.

'Good thinking.' I could tell that George was still a little jealous of Pickles and Harold was his friend, he didn't want to risk losing him to Pickles. I knew that wouldn't happen, Harold doted on George, but I didn't say anything. George had to figure that one out for himself.

I was left alone in the house, and again, that was a nice moment for me. I thought that I'd go and hang out with neighbourhood cats later, but for now, I could take some time for myself. As I went to find Jonathan's cashmere blanket, I was pretty pleased with myself.

It was a little chilly as I made my way to the recreation ground later, to see if any of the cats were around. Rocky was there, sitting in his usual spot, along with Nellie. There was no sign of Elvis.

'Hey guys,' I said as I joined them.

'Alfie, lovely to see you,' Rocky said.

'And you too. So what's new?' I asked, but before they could reply, I spotted Salmon looming towards us. Salmon lived opposite us with the Goodwins, leaders of the Edgar Road neighbourhood watch. They were busybodies, as was their cat. We'll never be best friends but we're civil.

'Hi, Salmon,' I said. Salmon liked to lord it over us when there was news or gossip on the street.

'Hello. What's going on?' he asked.

'Nothing much,' I replied. 'Is there anything you know that we don't?' I preempted him.

'No, it's been really quiet at the moment. Which is good because I can report there are no criminals on the street.'

'That is good,' Nellie said, she sounded a little sarcastic.

'But don't worry, we are keeping our eyes open just in case,' Salmon said, self-importantly. I didn't want to upset him, although he was a little silly.

'We're lucky to have you, Salmon,' I said, kindly, as Nellie and Rocky shot me a look. Before we could continue, George ran up to us with Elvis at his heels.

'Goodness me you can run,' Elvis said, he sounded a little out of breath.

'What's the emergency?' Nellie asked. George ground to a halt but couldn't speak. I looked upon him with concern while he calmed down.

'It's bad, Dad,' he said, his eyes full of concern, when he recovered.

'Oh no, what's happened?' I felt panic in my fur.

'Harold. When we got there, he said he wasn't feeling too good. So Claire phoned the doctors, but he started breathing funny, and they said he might need an ambulance, so Polly called for one. When it came, they examined him and said they thought it might be his heart, so they took him to hospital. Claire went in the ambulance with him, as they wouldn't let me go with them, but Polly was still there.' He lay down, exhausted. I nuzzled him.

'Oh George, I'm so sorry, but Harold is going to the best place. Remember before when he went to the hospital, he came back right as rain,' I pointed out, going to comfort George.

'But he looked so scared, and I wanted to go with him because I know that would make him feel better, but they wouldn't let me. They said cats weren't allowed to go in ambulances,' he huffed.

My poor boy was so distressed. 'But I know he wanted me with him, Dad, because he told me how I was his best friend in the world,' George cried.

'Right, George, let's find Polly and stick with her, because it's the best way for us to hear any news as soon as she gets it.'

'I think she's at her house, she said she'd go there to make phone calls,' George said, still clearly in a state.

'Come on, son, we'll go there. Guys, we'll come back and let you know as soon as there's any news,' I offered.

'Let us know if we can do anything,' Rocky shouted after us as we left them to go to Polly's.

Inside the house, Polly was on the phone. She hung up and saw us.

'Ah, boys, are you alright?' she said.

'Yowl,' George cried, no he wasn't.

'I know it was frightening. Claire is at the hospital with Harold now, and there's no news yet, but she'll let us know. I phoned Marcus, who is going straight there, and I've also let Matt know. Unfortunately, all we can do now is wait.' I loved how Polly also spoke to us as if we were humans, it meant we always knew what was going on. Pickles was asleep in his bed, snoring gently, which was probably for the best for now, because I wasn't sure how patient George would be with him.

George placed himself at Polly's feet, there was no way he was going to leave her side for now. I gave him a little space. I knew George. If I fussed too much, it would annoy him. I said a prayer in my head that Harold would be alright. George had suffered enough loss in his short life so far, and I didn't want this for him. If I could have done anything to protect him, I would have done so, but for now, I was utterly helpless.

It was a very long, difficult afternoon. Every time the phone rang, George jumped up, and when there was no news, he put his head in his paws and fretted.

'What is an ambulance?' Pickles asked me when he woke up, and I herded him away from George.

'When you were little, you went to the vet to have injections,' I started to explain. 'And the hospital is where humans go for things like that.' I knew it was better to keep it simple.

'So, the old man . . . '

'Harold is his name, Pickles. He's George's best friend, and he isn't well, so it's best to give George some space.'

'I can try,' Pickles said. 'But I don't really understand.'

'Of course not, it's a lot for a puppy like you to take in, don't worry.' I didn't know if I had the energy to reassure everyone right now, but clearly I would have to because there was no one else to do so.

'OK, Alfie, if you say don't worry then I won't worry. Can I go and play with my ball now?'

'Good idea.'

Thankfully the children had been teaching Pickles the joy of playing with a tennis ball, which is something that cats see as being beneath them. Pickles would wait for them to throw it and chase it, bringing it back to them over and over again. Which kind of highlighted the difference between dogs and cats, but if it made him happy . . . I went with him, in order to give George the space he needed, and I batted the ball with my paw, so he could chase it. It was a little tiresome but I was trying hard not to complain as I batted it yet again.

There was still no news of Harold when Polly had to go to pick up the children. She took Pickles, on his lead, but poor George still didn't know what to do with himself. He was so distressed.

'Do you want to go and see Hana?' I suggested.

'That's a good idea. Hana might know something, or Sylvie might be there . . .'

'And if I get any news I will come right round straight away, I absolutely promise,' I said.

'You're right, Dad, at least it'll be better than sitting here just worrying.'

'And you know Hana might be worried too, I mean she's almost related to Harold now as well,' I pointed out.

'Oh, poor Hana, I was too busy worrying about myself, but she might need me. Oh, how could I not have realised that.' He sped off out of the house and yet again I was alone.

I paced up and down until Polly came home, the children all bounded in, and when she had settled them with snacks and drinks, she picked me up.

'No news, sorry, mate,' she said, stroking my fur. I didn't know whether to go to George or wait with Polly, but in the end, I decided to wait. Because if George had any news he'd come and find me, and if I got news first I could go and find him, which meant we had all bases covered. All we could do was wait.

Polly had bathed and put the children in pyjamas, settling them on the sofa when Matt got home from work, and shortly after Claire arrived with Jonathan.

'What a day,' Claire said as she kissed the children.

'How's Harold?' Matt asked.

'He's going to be alright, but he's got a bit of recovery time ahead of him. It's his heart, not a heart attack, thank goodness, but it's got some blockage or something, so they're keeping him in to do tests and take it from there. Marcus was really upset when he arrived, luckily Sylvie came straight afterwards, which reminds me I need to go to hers and wait for Connie to come home, she called her and she's upset too. Jon, will you be OK putting the kids to bed?'

'Of course, darling.' He gave her a hug. 'Don't worry. See what Connie wants, she might want to stay at hers rather than come to us.'

'Which makes sense, look, we're all here to help out, let's just keep in touch,' Polly said.

Everyone scattered and I went with Claire to find George.

Claire let herself in with the spare key, and found Connie at the kitchen table, in tears. Hana was on her lap, George at her feet. I rushed to George and nuzzled him as we listened to Claire explain to Connie what she knew.

'But can I see him?' Connie asked. After all, Harold was like a surrogate granddad to her. He was a gruff old man but very loving to Sylvie and Connie.

'Sorry, love,' Claire said. 'They're doing tests right now, but your mum will be back soon, and I think even Marcus will be kicked out, so your mum said to tell you that you can visit him tomorrow.'

'Meow?' George asked hopefully, but I didn't think he could. Cats didn't go to hospitals, I was pretty sure.

'I guess I'll wait then. I've got homework to do, Claire, I better go and do it in my room.'

'I'll wait here, until your mum gets home then. Can I get you something to eat, love?'

'No, thanks, I had a sandwich earlier, but really I don't have an appetite.'

Hana followed Connie upstairs, George hot on her paws. I climbed into Claire's lap.

'He'll be alright, Alfie,' Claire said, as she stroked me, but her voice was not full of conviction. 'I'm sure he'll be back to his cantankerous ways before we know it.' Harold could be quite grumpy, but George seemed to love that about him. And since we'd all become friends, we were used to him.

He had to get better. George couldn't lose someone else he loved, not so close to losing Tiger. And for that matter, neither could I.

Chapter
Eleven

It was a bad night for us all. George barely slept, he padded from Toby's room to my bed and back again a number of times. Marcus phoned late last night when he got back from the hospital to say that Harold was comfortable and that the doctors didn't feel that there was any immediate danger. It was more a case of keeping him calm, regulating his heart, while they got to the bottom of things. All we could do was stay calm and keep our paws crossed, although poor George kept worrying and as he kept waking me, I hoped they found out what was wrong with him sooner rather than later. Otherwise, none of us were going to get any sleep. I also tried to reassure him, but as George pointed out, I wasn't a doctor, so my words didn't soothe him.

All the adults discussed the situation at length and were all saying how the next few days would be chaotic, but of course, we were used to chaos. From what I could tell, until they had the test results, all my humans would be on edge, as well as us. Most importantly, they wanted to protect the children until they knew the situation, which I couldn't do with George as he knew too much. The younger ones didn't really understand, so my focus was to keep Pickles out of trouble and support George.

That morning, as Claire took the children off to school, Pickles was once again in our care. George wanted, and needed, to go to Hana's so I was on puppy-sitting duty. Even though I didn't exactly have the energy, I wondered if it would be safe to try to play hide and seek again. I just had to hope he didn't get stuck in a cereal packet again. Thankfully George had shown him the best (safest) hiding places, under Summer's bed was the best, which Pickles seemed to like, and there was no danger involved. For now, while everyone worried about Harold, I helped out by taking care of Pickles.

'Alfie, can I have something to eat?' Pickles asked. Now I was a cat who liked their food, pilchards especially, but this puppy wanted to eat all the time. His stomach was bottomless, and he did have a rather large bottom.

'Pickles, you've had your breakfast so there's nothing until lunchtime,' I told him, sounding like a parent. 'You need to do something other than eat.' I tried to be stern, but when he looked at me with those big, hopeful eyes, it was difficult not to melt and give him all the food in the house. Until he licked my ear, which I really didn't like.

'Can I have some of your food?' he asked, wiggling his bottom hopefully.

'You don't like it, and besides, George and I ate all our breakfast today,' I said. Ever since Pickles entered our lives, we had quickly learnt not to leave food in our bowls.

'Right, so are you saying that I can't have anything to eat?' This puppy really did labour the point.

'Let's go to the garden,' I suggested thinking it might get rid of some of his energy. We headed out the cat flap. The wind whipped through our fur the moment we stepped outside.

'It's chilly,' Pickles said, shivering.

'Shall we play hide and seek?' I suggested.

'Oh yes please, yes please.'

'Great, you hide, and I'll count to twenty.'

'No, Alfie, twenty isn't enough time for me to hide, count to five.'

Bless, he still hadn't got the hang of numbers. I did wonder if he'd get smarter as he got older, but George didn't think he would. I was still optimistic, that was the kind of cat I was. I decided to just turn my back while he hid, after all in the garden there weren't many places. Within a matter of seconds, I turned around and felt a quick flutter of panic when I couldn't see him anywhere. I moved down the small lawn towards the shed, which looked as if it was shut so he couldn't be in there. I saw a big pile of leaves, and a tail wagging from one edge. I actually felt quite proud, it was his best hiding place yet.

'Pickles, I've found you,' I shouted and then laughed as leaves scattered everywhere and he emerged.

'Shall we go inside?' I said, feeling increasingly chilled in my fur.

'Only if we can keep playing.' He ran ahead and into the house.

I lay down and had forty winks, which I think was enough time for Pickles to hide and then I got up, stretched, and set off upstairs. I looked under Summer's bed, but he wasn't there. So much for George's lesson. I went into Toby's room, but there was no sign of him there. Same with Claire and Jonathan's and I checked the bathroom too. I started to panic, but then I heard a gentle bark. Pickles' bark wasn't aggressive or scary, and I quite liked it. I followed the sound and found myself back in Toby's room. Then I saw Pickles. He had somehow got up onto the top bunk of Toby's bed. Oh no, I'm sure that George hadn't taught him to go there. And also how did he get up there?

'How did you get up there?' I asked. Toby had a ladder to the top bunk, the ladder rungs were quite thick, more like steps really, but still, although George and I could get up easily, I wasn't sure how that puppy had managed it with his short legs.

'I climbed up,' he announced proudly. 'I went slowly, and it seems that my legs growed so it wasn't easy, but it wasn't impossible either.'

'Maybe you are getting better at climbing,' I mused, although I worried that he could have fallen and hurt himself and that would have been my fault, so I didn't want to encourage him. After all, I was the adult, and I was supposed to be in charge.

'Yes, I really am. But I don't know how to get down,' he said. I looked and thought about it. I climbed up to join him. I didn't like to go up there, although I had done a couple of times, because heights weren't my favourite things, and this was higher than I found comfortable. 'How about you watch me get down and try to copy,' I suggested as I carefully reached the rungs and made my way down. I hoped the old adage would be right, if you can get up, then you can get down again. But my problem was the down bit. I tried to remain calm, hoping my legs didn't tremble and give me away, but I didn't like it at all.

Pickles came to the edge of the bed and stretched out a paw which didn't reach the next rung down. He squealed, shot back and landed on his tail.

'Ouch,' he squealed. 'I am not coming down, no way, that's too scary.' I sighed and tried to work out what to do. What were my options? I could go up again, but I wasn't big enough to carry him down, which is the only thing I could think of. In fact, he would be more likely to carry me these days.

'I thought George taught you to hide under beds?' I asked.

'Yes, he did but then I thought I would use my own ideas and try up here. I just didn't think about how to get down again.'

'Perhaps in future, you might not want to use your own ideas,' I said, as I sat down to think. After drawing several blanks, I realised, the only way to get Pickles down was with the help of an adult.

'You'll have to wait there until Claire comes home,' I said.

'Will you stay with me because I'm scared,' he said. My heart went out to him as his voice shook, and he appeared sad. He was still so young, and we all got in scrapes after all. I'd had my fair share over the years.

'Of course, I will.' I felt bad for him, I knew what it was like to be scared, it wasn't pretty. 'I'll be right here,' I reassured.

'No, Alfie, can you wait with me up here?'

I had no choice as I climbed up the ladder again while we waited for Claire to come home. Pickles kept nestling closer to me, until he was practically on top of me. He might be a baby, but he was quite heavy as I tried to liberate my tail from underneath him.

'I won't have to be here forever, will I?' he asked, in a smaller voice than normal.

'No, Pickles, Claire will be back soon, and she'll get you

down, don't worry,' I reassured him as we settled down to wait, silently wishing we were back in the pile of leaves.

'Stay there, I'll be right back I promise,' I said as soon as I heard the front door open after what felt like hours later.

'But don't be too long,' he called after me as I made the treacherous journey down the bunk bed steps again.

'Right, Alfie, I'll make your lunch. Where's George? Where's Pickles?' Claire asked as I greeted her. I brushed myself against Claire's legs, yowled a lot and got her to follow me upstairs. When she saw Pickles on the bed, her face was a picture.

'How on earth did you get up there?' she asked. She looked at me with a puzzled expression. I blinked at her.

'Woof,' he replied. Thankfully, she climbed straight up and lifted him down, and I hoped that he had learnt another lesson, another thing to avoid. Looking after Pickles was turning my grey fur even greyer.

Over lunch, which Pickles devoured greedily, Claire phoned Jonathan and told him that there was still no news about Harold, but the doctors had thankfully ruled out anything life-threatening. It was a relief, and Claire cried, as she spoke. I went and sat with her. But I knew that I needed to tell George because he needed this update more than anyone.

I cleaned myself up to go out.

'Where are you going?' Pickles asked.

'To find George,' I replied.

'Can I come with you?' he asked.

'No, Pickles, you need to stay with Claire, after all, you're not allowed out of the garden on your own.'

'But I wouldn't be on my own, I'd be with you.'

'I mean without a human adult,' I clarified.

'There are far too many rules for me to keep track of,' Pickles huffed.

I was out of the cat flap and by the back gate before I realised that Pickles had defied me by following me.

'Pickles, you need to go back.'

'I'm coming with you. I want to see George,' he whined.

'But Claire will worry if she can't find you and we really don't need any more stress,' I tried to reason, but reasoning with a puppy, it's not easy.

'We'll be back before she even notices,' he persisted.

I was faced with a dilemma. I needed to find George, to give him the news, and I didn't want to take Pickles, but if I went home, then I would have to try to sneak out again without him noticing, which I wasn't sure I could. I had made a promise to George that as soon as there was news I would deliver it, come what may. Or should I say, come what Pickles?

I hoped I wasn't going to regret this, and I decided I would just go for it. I slid under the gate with ease and stood on the other side. Within seconds Pickles appeared. I groaned, this wasn't what I had in mind. Maybe, just maybe I could get back before anyone noticed? I crossed my paws and carried on. After all, we were just popping next door. What could go wrong?

'See, I am just like a cat,' he said with a grin on his very dog-like face.

'Oh God, this isn't going to end well,' I sighed as I made my way to Hana's house. I slid through the cat flap and Pickles followed me, although it took him a bit longer, as it was a slightly different set-up to what he was used to. We found Hana and George in the living room.

'What on earth is that?' Hana asked as Pickles bounded in, wagging his bottom.

'That is Pickles. What is he doing here?' George replied.

'Hey, guys, do you want to play ball?' Pickles asked. Hana and George exchanged withering looks.

'Sorry, George, Claire just spoke to Jonathan about Harold. He is out of danger, stable but they just need to do some more tests, but the good news is that they have ruled out anything serious.'

'Oh that is good news. Why is your face like that?' Hana asked, still studying Pickles.

'It just is,' George replied. 'So when will Harold be home?' George asked.

'I don't know, it might be a while yet, but the important thing to remember is that it isn't serious, or life-threatening.'

'Thanks for telling me, Dad. Although I still don't know why he's here.'

'He followed me and I thought giving you the news about Harold was more important than trying to get him to do what I told him.'

'What now, though?'

'I better get him home before Claire notices that we've gone. Are you going to stay here, or come with us?' I asked.

'I'll come,' George sighed. 'Someone needs to keep that puppy in line. I'll come back later, Hana,' he said. They nuzzled, and we set off.

We were just outside our house when I heard George yowl.

'Pickles, no,' he shouted, his eyes frozen in horror. It was as if everything went into slow motion; Pickles had run into the road and was spinning round in circles, but a car was approaching.

'Pickles, get back here,' I shouted.

'Why?' he asked, not remotely in any kind of hurry to do as he was told, yet again. Panic filled my body, and before I even had time to think or knew what I was doing, I launched myself into the road, in front of him. I lay down and put my paws over my head and hoped for the best. A horn blasted, brakes screeched, and it all went quiet. I didn't feel anything hurting, I wasn't sure I could feel anything at all. Was this it? Had I gone too far this time? How could I have done this to my George? I felt my fur shaking in the wind, and my legs started shaking underneath me. I was still alive, and I didn't seem to have any pain.

'Dad,' George said, bounding over and breaking the silence, he sounded worried. I opened my eyes and blinked at my son. I was fine, the car had stopped inches from me. Pickles was standing still for once, although he didn't seem to understand what was going on. The driver rushed out of her car and leant down to pick me up.

'Are you alright?' she asked, panic lacing her voice.

'Meow.' My voice shook, but by some miracle I was. I was fine. As was Pickles. My impulsive behaviour had turned out OK. Thank goodness. I felt relieved, even if I was a bit shaken up.

Our front gate sprang open, and Claire appeared.

'What on earth is going on?' she shouted.

'The puppy ran into the road, and the cat seemed to throw

itself in front of it,' the lady explained, she was shaking but holding onto me tight. 'I wasn't going fast so thankfully I could stop in time, but I was practically touching him.' The driver burst into tears.

'Oh, goodness, I'm so sorry, I don't know how he got out. Pickles you do not go out without me. How many times do I have to tell you?' Claire had tears in her eyes now. 'Alfie, are you OK?'

'Meow.' I was almost fine.

'Alfie, you shouldn't have let Pickles come out, what were you thinking?' Sorry, sorry, are you alright?' She turned to the woman.

'Just a bit shaken up but I'm so relieved no one got hurt.'

Claire took us and the quivering lady into the house and sat her down in the kitchen. Claire made her a cup of tea, to help her calm down. Pickles, finally noticing he was in trouble, crawled straight into his bed.

George and I sat down, trying to calm ourselves. We were all trying to calm ourselves actually.

'I've never seen anything like it,' the lady, who told Claire she was called Sally, said. 'A cat throwing itself into the road to save the dog! I mean I know humans do that but cats?' She was genuinely confused.

'I'm guessing you've never met a cat like Alfie before,' Claire replied.

Chapter
Twelve

It was the end of a very stressful week. After the incident with the car, Claire told me off quite a lot. George also told me off for risking myself when he needed me. I know he had a point, but I tried to explain that I knew what I was doing and if I had been hit it would have been only a gentle bump. In reality, I knew nothing of the sort, and I felt guilty for putting him through it. I should have thought first and acted second. The trouble was that it was instinct rather than a thought out move, and because of that, I couldn't be sure I wouldn't do it again if faced with the same situation.

George and I both tried to hammer home to Pickles the seriousness of the situation.

'Pickles, can't you see how bad it was?' George said exasperated.

'Not sure,' Pickles replied.

'Listen to me,' I said, with my best stern parent voice. 'You could have been badly hurt, Pickles, and I could have been badly hurt. The point is that it was very bad, and you simply cannot do it again.'

'Alright, I think I get it, you are basically saying I shouldn't go into the road on my own?'

'We're saying you never go into a road on your own but also you shouldn't go out on your own,' I reiterated for what felt like the millionth time.

'I think I've got it, but you know I can't be sure,' Pickles replied. George stomped off, I despaired and Pickles licked his nose. He was never going to get it.

In hindsight I should have taken Pickles home, got Claire's attention and then gone to see George. But I was so keen for him to know Harold was alright, I made a mistake. I hold my paws up to it, I really do. No cat is perfect, after all.

And Claire was more cross with herself, but it was hard with everything going on. She was taking care of the house, the children, Pickles and also visiting Harold every day. What with Jonathan not coming home until late at night, she was on her own a lot. So I took the lectures with good grace as I knew what she was going through.

Harold's illness had definitely disrupted our calm almost more than Pickles. Marcus was worried, in fact, it was unclear who was the most upset, him or George. However, Marcus could go and see Harold, whereas George was getting increasingly annoyed about the fact that he couldn't. It turned out that Harold would be in hospital for quite a while longer by the sounds of things. They weren't going to operate but they had to try different medication and that could take some time to get right. There were lots of technical terms being bandied about, but I'm a cat, so I had no idea what most of it meant. The adults kept reassuring us (and themselves it seemed) that it was all going to be fine, and they all went to visit him, reporting back. I, in turn, tried to reassure George.

The good news was that Harold was complaining about the food, about the company – a bunch of ill old men he called them, and the nurses who were incompetent, and the doctors even worse. He seemed to think they were trying to kill him. Jonathan said it was a good sign, the fact he was well enough to moan suggested he was recovering. Despite my attempts at reassurance, George still fretted – he loved Harold.

'I miss Harold,' George said to me as we ate our breakfast. 'I feel as if it's been such a long time since I've seen him and he's one of my best friends.'

'I know, but the important thing is that he's doing well. How about I take you out today to cheer you up. We could go and see Dustbin?' I watched George's mind whirring as he thought about my offer. He was tempted, I could see, but he was also still a little angry with me about the car incident. 'No Pickles, I promise,' I added, the pilchard on the cake.

'OK, it's been ages since I saw Dustbin,' he said. 'But you have to guarantee that the dog does not follow us.'

'Great, you might get to meet Ally as well. So, George, let's go now before Polly arrives with Pickles. That way, there is no way he can try to follow us.'

'Good thinking, Dad. And it'll be nice, just the two of us again. I love it when it's the two of us.'

'Aye, son, I've missed that.' I felt quite emotional, as we headed out.

It was a clear day, cold but dry, as we headed towards the restaurant. I hoped we might get to see Franceska too, with the whole Pickles arrival I had been at home far more than usual and hadn't been out to see anyone as much. And although she had been to ours, since Harold having gone into hospital, I missed her. The adults had drawn up a roster of visiting Harold. Marcus went every evening, and in the afternoon when he could juggle work, Sylvie joined him in the evenings, taking Connie sometimes. Claire would go in the afternoon before the school run. Franceska would take over from her, while she went to get the children. Jonathan, Matt, Tomasz and Polly would all pop in after work just to show their faces.

Harold said he had the most visitors out of everyone, according to Claire. He was proud of this fact. Everyone wanted him to know he was loved, so although not everyone visited him every day, they visited a fair bit. Which only served to annoy George even more, as he felt he was the only one who didn't get to see Harold. Apart from the children and me. They didn't go because Claire said it would be too disruptive to the other patients, goodness, imagine if George or Pickles were allowed to visit in that case!

We set off. I did feel a little guilty about abandoning Pickles, but I had done a fair bit of puppy-sitting lately, and I seemed to get told off for every little thing he did wrong. Not only for the car business, but also when he dug up some flowers in Claire's garden, chewed one of Toby's trainers, buried one of Summer's dolls in the garden, ate something he shouldn't. The list went on, and I felt a little bit offended that it was all my fault. After all, puppy sitting was much harder than even I imagined. Harder even than when George was a kitten if my memory serves. I think I had earned an hour or two off. In reality, I'd probably earned a two week holiday, but that wasn't going to happen.

'You know I do like Pickles a bit,' George said magnanimously. 'But I also miss it being just us.'

'I do too, things change so much, don't they, maybe we should make sure we make time for each other,' I suggested.

'Yes, but I better warn you,' George said as we trod the familiar path to Dustbin, 'I am going to be very busy soon because I am close to finding my job.'

I raised my whiskers in surprise. 'Really? What is it?'

'Oh that I don't exactly know, but you have to trust me when I say that I am going to be very good at it.'

'I do trust you.' I really didn't. I worried about him, especially when I had no idea what he was going to be doing. Although to be fair, I wasn't sure he did either.

'Good, because you need to be able to give me some space to follow my dreams.'

'Eh?' I was confused, and had no idea what he was talking about.

'Thanks, Dad.'

'You're welcome, son.'

Thankfully our difficult conversation came to an end as we reached the restaurant.

We bumped into Franceska and Tomasz, as we padded through to the back of the restaurant.

'Ah, we haven't seen you here for a long time,' Tomasz said, fussing us both as he usually did.

'Alfie, George, I will get you some treats,' Franceska said. I rubbed against her legs in thanks.

'I have to go now, but it was nice to see you,' Tomasz said, before he took off, swinging his car keys. We waited by the back door of the restaurant for Franceska to bring out some sardines which we both enjoyed very much. After polishing them off, we made our way to the bins to find our friend.

'Hello, what a nice surprise,' Dustbin said. I had to say I needed a bit of a double take. He looked a bit different. His fur was neater and shinier, and he was smiling in a way I hadn't seen before. Ally appeared from behind him. Ah, now that made sense. He was making more of an effort with his appearance now he was in love. That was sweet.

'Oh it's like a girl Dustbin,' George said before he could stop himself. 'Sorry, I didn't mean . . . Well, I did mean . . . I mean . . .'

'I think George was going to say that you and Dustbin are obviously similar in some ways, your job mainly, but he didn't mean any offence by it,' I explained.

'None taken. Nice to meet you, George, I've heard all about you. And Alfie, lovely to see you again.'

'Wow, it's really nice to meet you too,' George said. 'Are you as good at hunting as Dustbin?'

'I am,' Ally said.

'She really is,' Dustbin added proudly.

'Show me, show me!' George begged. George bounded after Ally, I hoped his career wouldn't take him in the direction of her and Dustbin, I didn't really have the stomach for that, but then I knew I would have to support him if that was what he decided.

'I heard them talking about Harold, how's the lad coping?' Dustbin asked when we were alone.

'It's hard for him, you know, but Harold is on the mend. He just seems to be so upset that he can't visit him.'

'Of course, after everything he's been through . . . but even I know cats aren't allowed in hospitals, so he's just going to have to be patient – excuse the pun – poor thing.'

'You know George isn't known for his patience, Dustbin. Anyway, how are you and Ally?'

'Yeah, good. I like her.'

For Dustbin, a cat of few words, and certainly fewer emotional outbursts, this was like a huge admission.

'Then I'm happy for you.' I grinned. 'They say love makes the world go round after all.'

'Stop with all that soppy stuff,' he grumbled, but I could see that he was smiling underneath it all. We had a lovely time in the yard. After Ally finished showing George her hunting skills, we all found a rare sunny patch to sit in and have a catch-up. As winter had officially announced its arrival we knew we were lucky to find it.

'I just want to be able to find my purpose in life,' George reiterated.

'Not catching rodents then?' Ally asked.

'No, I don't feel that it's best suited to my aptitude,' George said. I had no idea where he was getting this from, but I guessed it was Aleksy and Connie. 'You see, in order to find my cat calling I need to get the sense it's one hundred per cent right for me.'

'I can see that,' Dustbin said, humouring him. 'And to start with, what do you think your best skill is?'

I watched George as he thought about it, whiskers raised, seriously. He looked about him, and then at me.

'I think my best skill is making people happy,' he said. Well, he did do that, that was true.

'In that case, you need to find a job where you make people happy,' Ally said.

'But what job involves that?' I asked.

'That's what we need to find out,' Dustbin said.

'No, I know it.' George suddenly sprang up. 'I know it. Thanks, Dustbin, Ally, you've really helped.'

'What is it?' I asked, being caught up in his excitement but also confused.

'I can't tell you that it'll take a bit of working out, but trust me, I think I have finally found my purpose in life.'

Should I be worried that he wouldn't share it with me? Probably, but I would just have to wait and see. And hope that it was nothing that could get him into trouble. What was I even saying? Of course, it would be something which got him into trouble. And probably get me into trouble too.

As soon as we slid through the cat flap, Pickles appeared and waddled up to us. In the few weeks he'd been here, he had got a bit bigger. Or wider, although he still could get through the cat flap, but I wasn't sure he would be able to for much longer. That might make life easier.

'Where have you been?' Pickles demanded.

'Urgent cat business,' George replied, self-importantly. I glared at him.

'Pickles, we needed to go out and see some friends of ours, but we tried to be as quick as we could,' I said trying to placate him.

'But I wanted to come,' he whined.

'You can't go everywhere with us,' I said gently. 'Remember what happened yesterday?'

'No,' he replied.

'You nearly got run over, and you nearly got Dad run over. It's dangerous out there, especially with your lack of road sense,' George huffed. He sounded angry, but this didn't seem to resonate with Pickles.

'Why?' he asked. Oh goodness, I remembered the why phase with George, it was an endless round of 'why?' questions and I wasn't sure I wanted to go through it again.

'Because,' George said, 'you are not a cat.'

'But you said if I did what you told me then I would be able to be a cat,' Pickles said. I tried not to put my head in my paws and weep.

'Yes, but it takes a very long time to be like me, years in fact,' George continued.

'George, shush,' I commanded, having to step in here. 'Pickles, you are very lucky to have George to teach you how to be a cat. But, there are some things you can't do, because of your own safety and one of those things is going out without a human.'

'Why?'

'When you go out, you have to have a lead on, well when you're not in the garden, right?' I explained.

'Yes.'

'George and I don't have leads on, cats don't and before you say why you need to know it's the fundamental difference between dogs and cats. Now, you can come and play with us in the garden, but when we go out, if we go out, you can't come with us.'

'It's not fair,' Pickles reiterated.

'Life isn't always fair,' George said, sounding wise. 'But, Pickles, that doesn't mean you can't have fun, but it's dangerous out there, beyond the garden gate, you need to remember that.'

I gave George a surprised look, I was surprised but pleased at how nice he was being.

'OK, but will you play with me now?' he asked.

'Dad will, I have to go out,' George said, and before I could question him about it, he was gone, and I was left with the puppy yet again.

I led Pickles to the garden, after a bit of a wiggle through the cat flap. I was tired after my morning's exertions, and I would have liked to have a quick cat nap, but it wasn't to be, as I had a puppy to entertain. We found some balls, which Pickles buried and then dug up. I tried not to look as he made a little bit of a mess of the garden. I'd probably be in trouble again, but I didn't have the energy to prevent it. I lay down and tried to watch Pickles, but I found it hard to keep my eyes open, and at some point, I must have dropped off.

'What on earth? Pickles, Alfie.' Claire's voice, which was full of anger, yet again, woke me and I jumped up. Pickles was sat at Claire's feet, looking very innocent. I stretched and went over.

'What have you done?' Claire shouted, again, pointing at the flowerbeds, which I had to admit were a bit of a mess. Of course, it was my fault, I should have been watching him, as I looked at the flowers, which Claire loved too much, scattered all over the lawn. Oh god, I was supposed to be the responsible adult here.

'Meow,' I apologised and hung my head. I felt a little bit guilty, but I was still also tired.

'Pickles, you have to stop digging up my flowers.' Claire picked him up, turned and glared at me. 'And, Alfie, you should have stopped him from doing so.' She took him inside. As the door closed behind them I thought about following them, but then I lay down again, thinking I also could just snatch another forty winks. It would beat being told off again, after all, I'd been told off enough lately.

Chapter Thirteen

'Do I have to go?' Jonathan asked as he took off his tie and jacket and tried to sit down on the sofa. Claire tried to stop him from sitting down and she didn't look best pleased.

'Jonathan, I know you're tired, but we haven't spent any time together this week, and I've been looking forward to this,' Claire snapped. 'Besides, Polly is coming to babysit for us, and it would be embarrassing to tell her that date night is off because my husband doesn't want to spend time with me.' I felt bad for her; Claire was wearing a lovely dress, she had spent quite a lot of time on her hair, and was wearing make-up. She'd been so excited as she tucked the children up in bed, and then gone to get ready. I went over to Jonathan and gave his leg a gentle scratch.

'Ow!' he shouted, glaring at me. 'You're ganging up on me now!' I did feel a bit guilty, but he needed to make an effort with his wife. I wanted to tell him I understood tiredness, after all, I'd fallen asleep when I should have been looking after Pickles. But of course, I couldn't.

'I made so much effort,' Claire added.

'Sorry, darling,' he said as the penny dropped. I did stand on his foot a couple of times to help him. 'You look gorgeous,' he finally said as he wrapped his arms around her. 'I'll get changed very quickly, and we will go and have a lovely dinner,' he promised.

'Thank you. I know you're tired, love, but what with the

house and visiting Harold, the kids, I feel as if I haven't spent any time with you and I also could really do with getting out of the house.'

'I know and I'm sorry. I guess our lives are so different now with you doing all the house stuff, I don't think enough about your day . . .'

'And I don't always appreciate how hard you're working either. Let's make a pact to work at us, as much as I work on the family, and you work in the office,' Claire said, nuzzling into her husband.

'I love you.' He kissed her. 'Right give me five minutes to freshen up, and then we'll have the best dinner ever.' He grinned.

'Alfie, thanks for your support.' Claire picked me up and cuddled me as Jonathan went to get changed. It seemed I was forgiven now, too.

Polly rushed in and immediately gave me a squeeze. It would be nice to spend a bit of time with her, just the two of us, which was rare. When Claire and Jonathan left, Polly and me snuggled up on the sofa together, and settled down for the evening.

When Polly's phone rang, interrupting our peace, I jumped up.

'Hey, Matt,' Polly said. I climbed on Polly's lap and tried to listen.

'I just spoke to Marcus, Harold had a relapse, he's not reacting to the drugs as they hoped, and so he's quite poorly. Marcus is with him tonight, and Sylvie will phone you with any news, but he sounded pretty devastated.'

'Oh no, I thought he was on the mend. Please tell me that he's not critical. Should I get Claire and Jon home?'

124

'No, honey, he's not critical, but he's not too good either. I just wanted to let you know. And I told Marcus we'd go to the hospital tomorrow if that's OK?'

'Of course, and if he calls again find out if we can take anything with us.'

After Polly hung up, she stroked me, and I wondered how I would break the news to George. He was asleep with Toby, so I thought I would wait until the morning and tell him then. I didn't know how George would react, and I wasn't sure it was fair for me to sugar-coat the news, so I had to find a gentle way of telling him the truth without scaring him.

The following day, I was awake early, fretting about how I would tell George that Harold was still poorly. I kept reassuring myself that he was going to be fine. I just hoped he was.

'Morning, Dad.' George joined me in the kitchen.

'Oh hi, son, did you sleep well?' I asked.

'Yes, thanks, you're up early.'

'I know, George, listen I heard Polly talking to Matt last night, and it turns out that Harold might be in hospital a bit longer than we thought. He's alright, not serious, apparently, but he needs to get his medicine right before he can come home, so it might be a while.'

'But I haven't seen him for ages, Dad, and he's my friend.' George stamped his paw in anger.

'I am so sorry, George, but at least we're getting to hear all about what is happening. And Marcus is going to see him again this morning, and Polly and Matt will be there later, Sylvie will be going at some point so I am sure we will hear all about it.'

'But I want to see him.'

As everyone got ready for the day, the doorbell went. I followed Claire to the door, Marcus was stood on the doorstep.

'Hi, Marcus, so sorry to hear that Harold's still not too good,' Claire said.

'It was pretty scary, but he's in good hands and out of danger. They just need to adjust his medication, I honestly think he'll be fine, but I'm going to see him now, before work. I've got special dispensation because of the scare last night. Anyway, I just wondered if you would be able to pop in sometime today with clean pyjamas for him, I know you've got a key and Sylvie's working.'

'It's absolutely fine, I'll go as soon as visiting hours start if that's OK?'

'Yes please, I'm so grateful. I better go now.' Marcus gave Claire a quick hug and turned to go. I turned to speak to George, but he had already followed Marcus out the front door. I thought about getting out of the cat flap and going to follow him, but then I realised that he probably needed some time alone to cool off. It was hard being a parent. Before I could give the situation more thought, the door went again, Polly piled in with the children, followed by a bouncy Pickles.

'I just saw George, he looked as if he was going somewhere in a hurry,' Polly said, but before I could dwell on her words, Pickles bundled into me.

'Oi, be careful,' I said. 'You'll soon squash me as flat as a pancake.' Pickles was growing at an alarming rate it seemed, in width anyway.

'Oh and Claire, I know our puppy is greedy, but the vet said he's weighing a bit much for his age so he's on a diet and we need to make sure he gets more exercise.'

'Got it, I'll make sure there's no food left out. No cat food or human food,' she said, shooting me a look. Great, if Pickles was on a diet, did that mean I was too? 'I'm going to see Harold later, taking him some bits and pieces, so I'll call and let you know how he is.'

'Thanks, Claire. See you later, kids.' With a flourish, Polly was gone.

As Claire got the children ready to go to school, she turned to us.

'Right, Pickles, I'm going to take you with us, you need the exercise,' she said, clipping his lead on. 'Coming, Alfie?' I tilted my head to suggest I would. George and I often did the school run with her, we loved seeing where the children went, and the school wasn't too far away.

'Meow.' Don't mind if I do.

We walked together, the children taking turns with Pickles' lead, apart from when we crossed roads, because Claire took charge of everyone, she clearly wasn't taking any chances after the other day, not that she ever did. Toby picked me up and carried me across the roads. I didn't want to point out that I was capable and I could cross roads unaided in front of Pickles, so I let Toby carry me. When we got to the school gates, the children rushed in, greeting the teacher who was the playground monitor for the day, and then waving behind to us.

'Right then, home time,' Claire said. As she started to walk us home, Pickles managed to wrap his lead around my paws, causing me to fall over.

127

'Oh, Pickles,' Claire said, untangling us and then picking me up. Luckily I wasn't in too much pain from the accident, but I gave Pickles a little bit of a wide berth for the rest of the walk. When we got home, there was still no sign of George. I let Pickles follow me around the house, he said he needed to watch me to learn about being a better cat. I didn't even have the energy with everything that was going on to point out for what felt like the millionth time that he was a puppy. So I went about my usual cat business with him as my little shadow. I went to lie on my favourite blanket and I looked out of the window. But no matter how hard he tried, Pickles couldn't get up onto the windowsill, and I didn't have the heart to watch him try for too long. So I hopped off my perch so that we could take a walk around the garden. Perhaps I needed to make my cat activities more dog-friendly, or Pickles friendly anyway. There was still no sign of George, but I couldn't risk leaving the house to go and look for him. I hoped Claire would take Pickles for a walk to give me some space, but she had to go and get things for Harold, so once again I was left in charge. I know I was an adult, but I was also a cat, and the responsibility being piled on me was vast. However, I was flattered because clearly everyone felt that I could handle it and they were almost right.

'Right,' I said. 'Time to practise napping,' I said, as I led Pickles to curl up on the sofa with me. it had been a tiresome morning, and I needed some peace. Thankfully Pickles started snoring the moment he lay his head down, and I was ready to rest myself. I had to think about Harold, and what he might be going through – we all knew how much he hated hospital by now. I thought about George and the fact that he was frustrated by not being able to see Harold. I had to think about all my families, and I said a little prayer for everyone before I lay my head down and fell asleep – the little pug snoring next to me.

Chapter
Fourteen

After a restful cat nap, I woke up feeling uplifted for a change. It was girls' night, or rather ladies' night at our house and my favourite human women would all be under one roof. It was lovely being a friend to so many people, but when they were all together, my heart would swell with happiness. Since coming to Edgar Road, I had been incredibly busy, making friends, bringing people together and solving problems, so George was right, I did have a vocation, and so, therefore, I understood how important it was to him. I determined that I would help him with his quest. I might not have taken him as seriously as I should have done . . . But for now, I was going to hang out with my favourite bunch of women; Claire, Franceska, Polly and Sylvie.

I said goodnight to George, who although now old enough to stay up with us, wanted to go and be with Toby.

'That's fine, son, but you know where I am if you want me,' I said.

'Of course. But I need an early night, I'm exhausted,' he said, stretching his paws and yawning.

'Pickles kept you busy earlier, didn't he?' I had been quite pleased when George said he'd hang out with Pickles for a bit, so I could go out and see my friends. We still had to be careful because if we both went out, he followed us.

'Yeah it was fun, I was trying to teach him how to meow.'

'And how did that go?'

'Not great, whenever he tried it still came out as a woof, but it was quite funny.'

'Sweet dreams, son.' I gave him a quick nuzzle and then headed downstairs, chuckling to myself. Poor Pickles didn't stand a chance.

Jonathan had gone to Matt's to 'get out of the way', as he put it, but I was pleased; he'd been working so much lately he hadn't had time for any of us, including his friends. He and Matt were best friends, so it would do them good to spend a bit of time together. Again, thanks to yours truly. They did invite Marcus, but he was with his dad at the hospital, and he'd taken Connie with him to cheer Harold up. The children were tucked into bed, but I knew that Toby and George were not asleep but playing on Toby's tablet under the covers. I think Claire knew as well but was also turning a blind eye. We parents sometimes did that, we would choose our battles. Besides, it wasn't a school night, and therefore we could all have a lie-in the following day. Paws crossed.

'Dig in,' Claire said, as they sat at the kitchen table, all with glasses of wine and food laid out.

'It looks great, Claire, I am so hungry right now. Sometimes I think that working in a restaurant puts me off food,' Franceska said.

'Frankie, you work in the office,' Polly pointed out. They laughed.

'Yes, but I am around the food all day still,' Franceska argued. 'It's a good diet in a way.'

'Maybe I should come and work with you,' Sylvie said. 'I've put on a bit of weight lately.'

'Not that anyone can tell.' Polly rolled her eyes.

'It's because you're happy,' Claire pointed out. 'You are, aren't you?' Claire worried about Sylvie, I knew because she had had such a hard time, and meeting Marcus had been great for her, but with Harold at the hospital, it wasn't as peaceful as it had been, although they seemed to be coping well.

'I am. I wish they would sort out Harold though. Marcus is incredibly worried, naturally, and he's running himself ragged being at the hospital all the time. But you know, he's going to be there for longer than we hoped. Which isn't great for any of us.'

'It must be hard, well I know it's hard because fitting everything in including visiting Harold in hospital isn't easy,' Polly said.

'And you guys have been great, knowing that you're all visiting him takes some of the pressure off Marcus, but you know what he's like.'

'A lovely man,' Franceska said. She was a big fan of Marcus, in fact, we all were.

'It's funny because I still think of it as the early days in our relationship. We see each other a lot, but we haven't discussed the future yet, but you know I feel as if he's been there forever in some ways. And he's so different from my ex—'

'Don't go there,' Polly warned wagging a finger at Sylvie. They laughed.

'No, but you know he, my ex, really wants Connie to go to Japan for Christmas, and I know I won't be alone, but it would be the first Christmas I wasn't with my daughter since she was born.' She shuddered. 'And I've told them both, him and Connie that is, that it's her choice. The problem is I know she's conflicted.'

'She would be, do you think she wants to go?' Claire asked. I thought it would be sad to not have Connie here for Christmas, but I also knew that Connie missed her dad.

'I don't know. She's so loyal after the turmoil of last year she doesn't want to say, I've tried to tell her that I don't mind and that I'd be fine here with Marcus and all of you, but I don't know. She's not happy with her father, especially now he has a new family, but I also don't want her to cut him off. He is her dad, after all.'

'Do you want me to talk to Aleksy about it?' Franceska asked. 'I never ask him to betray her confidence, but I could say that we're worried she doesn't know what to do so maybe he could make sure she is OK?'

'That's a great idea, as long as you don't say it's come from me,' Sylvie said. 'Thanks, Frankie, I don't need to know what she says, but it would be great to know that she can confide in Aleksy.'

I would have suggested the same – I had taught my humans well.

'Gosh, can you believe we're talking about Christmas already?' Claire said. I couldn't believe it. It was late October, so actually, it wasn't that far away. It would be our second Christmas without Tiger who we lost in December last year. I felt emotion well up, I missed her. I would have given anything to see her one last time. Just as I was about to wallow, I felt a drop of something wet on my head. I jumped up and then onto Franceska's lap.

'Sorry, Alfie, I got carried away, and spilt my wine,' Polly said, looking guilty. Franceska wiped my fur and then stroked me as I settled down on her lap, purring.

'So what do you think, we should do a big Christmas again, like last year?' Polly asked.

'Not exactly like last year,' Claire laughed.

'Oh can we not talk about it yet, I have so much work to do because I like to take time off in December, but if I don't get it done then you'll have to do my shopping, Claire,' Polly laughed. It was a family joke that Claire loved shopping, a bit too much. Jonathan moaned about it all the time.

'You know I'd love that,' Claire replied. 'But you know, I'll have to do everything this year, because Jonathan's been tasked with heading up a department which has lost staff due to incompetence, so he needs to turn it around. He is also hiring staff, so when he finds the right people, in theory, it will take the pressure off him a bit.' Her eyes darkened slightly.

'Bear with it, Claire,' Franceska said. 'When we started out with the restaurants, remember how mad I got about never seeing Tomasz or him seeing the kids? But we sorted it out.'

'You went back to Poland and threatened not to come back,' Polly pointed out.

'Yes, I did, but that was because Tomasz didn't realise how much he was neglecting his family, which was different. Jon knows he's working too much and he's already trying to sort it out.'

I crossed my paws that he was.

'I know, and I've said that I will support him,' Claire said.

'But if it carries on into the new year then maybe I'll go to Poland.' They laughed again.

Their easy chatter was music to my ears. Life might not be perfect, never perfect, but still better than it could have been. And that was enough for this cat. For now.

Chapter
Fifteen

'Just where exactly are you going?' I asked George as he stood by the cat flap. I knew I sounded like an overbearing parent, but I didn't care. I was feeling suspicious.

'I'm going to see Hana,' he replied. I narrowed my eyes. It wasn't that I didn't believe him exactly, but I could tell he was hiding something. Also, it was very early, and he didn't usually go out this early.

'But her family might all still be asleep,' I pointed out. After all, ours was. It was a school day, or weekday, whatever the best term was, and I had noticed, from my bed, on the landing, George get up, quietly as if he didn't want to wake me as he crept downstairs. Something was definitely going on.

'No they get up super early,' he replied, confidently. 'Anyway, she needs a friend, because she's sad about Harold,' he continued.

I was confused, George was the one who was closest to Harold.

'But, aren't you sad about Harold?' I asked.

'Of course I am, but he's going to be fine. I know it.'

I surrendered, and let him go. 'Don't be too long,' I shouted after him, still unable to shake the feeling that there was something he wasn't telling me. I had to resist the urge to go after him, I knew that would cause a row between us but I also knew my kitten really well, and I knew when he was hiding something.

I paced around trying to think when Jonathan emerged. His hair was wet from the shower and he was in his dressing gown. Gosh, he was up earlier than usual too.

'What are you doing up?' he asked, echoing my thoughts.

'Meow.' Hoping for breakfast now, actually.

'Right, coffee's on, let's get you and George some breakfast.'

As Jonathan made his coffee and I made a start on my breakfast, it was nice for us to spend time together, just the two of us. Rare but welcome.

'Need to get into the office early, there are a few interviews for staff today, so it's looking hopeful that I might not be such an absent father and husband soon!' he told me. Jonathan sounded cheerful.

'Meow,' I reassured.

'I know, and I've given myself a deadline, by the new year I want my department fully staffed so I can still work hard but not the ridiculous hours I've been doing, and I'm pretty sure I can meet that deadline, actually,' he continued, taking a sip of his coffee and grimacing because I guess it was too hot.

'Yowl.' I'm right with you.

'It's going to be so much better for all of us, including me,' Jonathan said.

'Are you talking to Alfie or yourself?' Claire snuck up on us, taking us both by surprise.

'Alfie, of course, he's a great listener,' Jonathan said as Claire gave his cheek a kiss.

'Meow,' I responded. I really was.

After our early start, I was pleased when Claire said that

142

Pickles was going with her to do the school run. There was still no sign of George, so with the house empty I took advantage of having a bit of time to cat nap before the whirlwind that was Pickles returned. When George was a tiny kitten I would snatch sleep wherever I could, parenting tip number two, and I was now doing the same with Pickles. As I found a sunny spot on the sofa, which was getting rarer and rarer every day, I took my nap. I was woken by a wet nose pressed against mine.

'George?' I asked, before I realised I was half asleep.

'Oh wow, it's working, I'm getting to be like George,' Pickles said as I opened my eyes.

'Well, I think you're more like you,' I said, diplomatically. 'You need to find your own self you know, Pickles. You don't have to do everything George does.'

'I don't, he tried to teach me to chase birds yesterday but I couldn't jump up on the fence like he can,' he said sadly. 'In fact I can barely jump.'

'Oh dear, Pickles, you can't do everything like a cat, it's a matter of biology.' I had no idea if this was the right term but I wanted to sound as if I knew what I was talking about.

'But one day when I'm bigger?'

'No, Pickles, as much as it's fun to do some of the things George does, there are others which you absolutely must not. The first is going out without a human, the second is climbing.' I wondered what else would have to go on the list. I had a feeling it would be a very long list.

'It's not fair that I can't do all these fun things, to be honest. And Alfie, I'm sure you know what you're talking about a bit but I'm not sure you're right. I think in time and with practice I can definitely absolutely do everything that George does.'

Oh no, this wasn't going exactly as planned.

'You know not all cats like to climb, I'm not keen on it myself,' I continued.

'But I am and one day I'm going to be a climber.'

I didn't have the energy to argue further, but thankfully Claire came in, and to my surprise Marcus was with her.

'Right, sit down, and have a cup of tea, and then we'll go through everything,' Claire said.

'You really are a life saver. I really could do without having to go, but it was booked ages ago and it's work . . .'

'Marcus, you're going to Scotland not to outer space. Your dad isn't critical anymore, and I can visit him every morning after the school run, find out what he needs for the day, then take it in the afternoon. Sylvie is going to go in the evenings, and Polly, Matt and Jonathan will when they can too, we'll keep an eye on him.'

'Thanks, Claire, you know he's getting better because he's constantly moaning.'

'Oh yes, when I last saw him he accused one of the nurses of trying to kill him off.'

'How they haven't tried already I will never know,' Marcus laughed.

'You know he's going to be fine, don't you?'

'I do but he is getting older, and you know I live with him at the moment, but he might need more care before too long.' Marcus scratched his head, I wished he'd do the same to mine. I loved a good head scratch.

'Cross that bridge when you come to it, but, Marcus, he'll be fine, you're only gone for a few days.'

'I know, I know, but you understand the guilt. We take care of people, Claire, that's what we do.'

'Speaking of Sylvie,' Claire said.

'I wasn't,' Marcus replied but we both knew he was a bit.

'Really?' Claire raised an eyebrow.

'OK, I love her to bits, you know that, but I'm worried, she's been a bit moody lately, and I think it might be to do with the idea of Connie going to Japan for Christmas.'

'Is she going?'

'We don't know, we both spoke to her, and told her that she had our blessing but it was her decision. She hasn't mentioned it since, and Sylvie doesn't want to push. I think also being at the hospital so much takes its toll on both of us, as well, so maybe that's adding to it . . . But you know when I first met her she was upset, and since then she's always been so level-headed. However she might be having a bit of a relapse.'

'I'll have a chat with her, she said she was fine when she was over the other night, but I can double check.'

'Thanks, Claire, you are such a star, I do appreciate it.'

Did I now need to add Sylvie to the list of people I worried about?

'George.' I almost jumped on him the minute he got home.

'What's wrong?' he asked.

'Oh nothing, I just wondered how Sylvie was.'

'How should I know that?'

'I assumed you'd been with Hana today, after all she's your best friend.'

'Oh yeah, right, she said that Sylvie had been a bit grumpy lately but she didn't know why.' George seemed preoccupied. I hoped he hadn't had a falling out with Hana.

'What's wrong?'

'Apparently Sylvie said she felt tired and irritated a lot, and she didn't feel that good, it's not a big deal though.'

'Oh it isn't? That's a relief, I was worried for a minute.'

'Anyway, I haven't been with Hana all day.'

'But you've been out all day, George, where have you been?'

'Dad, I can't tell you, but trust me, I was only doing good. I was doing my job.'

'You were doing your job?'

'I suppose I was, actually. Yes, I was at work today.'

'The job you can't tell me about?'

'No, Dad, it's early days, so I think it's best to keep it to myself for now.'

'George, I am really confused about this.'

'I know, and I'm sorry but it's kind of a secret job and I can't tell anyone. Don't feel it's just you that I'm keeping it from, no one knows anything about it.'

He went off to get some food and I sat there, feeling flummoxed. Should I worry? Where had he been? I decided to go out myself and see if anyone else knew anything.

'Nellie, I'm so glad you're here, did you see George today?' My words gushed out as soon as I reached the recreation ground.

'Um no Alfie, but—'

'Oh goodness, where has he been? I mean he can't visit Harold's house, and he said he hadn't seen Hana since this morning. He seems to think he's got himself a job but everyone knows that cats don't really have jobs, so I have no idea.' I paced up and down, and barely noticed that my other friends, Rocky and Elvis, had approached Nellie. Even Salmon was there.

'What is it?' I asked looking between them. They all looked serious. 'Has something happened with George, is that what this is?' I asked, panicked. 'Is something wrong with him?'

'No, Alfie, although this does affect George,' Nellie said kindly.

'Can one of you tell me what's going on?' I demanded, this was scaring me. The way my friends were all looking at me wasn't great.

'OK,' Salmon said, glancing at the others. It had to be bad if they'd included him. 'I came to find you, and I told the others, because, you know my family is friends with the Barkers?' The Barkers were Tiger's family.

'Yes, so?' I had a bad feeling.

'Well, the Barkers have, there's no easy way to say this, Alfie, but they've got another cat.'

I felt the words stick in my throat. I wanted to yowl, but I knew that I couldn't do that. I had a million questions but I wasn't sure I wanted the answers. Tiger was irreplaceable.

'Right.' I sat down as if I'd been physically winded.

'Alfie, Tiger is not being replaced,' Rocky said, gently.

'But the Barkers were so lost without her, and it's been almost a year, so they thought it would be time. The cat they've got, Oliver, he's not a kitten and they can give him a good home,' Salmon said, sounding more compassionate than I ever heard him be in my life. I raised my whiskers. I knew that the Barkers would be lost without Tiger, and I knew that the cat flap never heralding her arrival home must have been painful for them. The same way seeing her window-sill empty was painful for us.

'Are you alright?' Nellie asked.

'I don't know,' I replied, honestly. 'Does George know?' This might explain things.

'No, as Nellie said, we haven't seen him all day and he didn't come this way, so I guess he didn't go past the Barkers' house,' Elvis said.

'What's the new cat like?' I asked. I felt deflated, horrible, but I still had to get all the information because George was going to have to know about this and I would be the one to tell him.

'As far as I know he's called Oliver, he came from a local shelter, because his owners couldn't have him anymore, but I don't know more than that.'

I felt terrible, because when I was homeless, I'd been too scared to go to the shelter, too young to understand that it was a safe place for cats so I had run away instead, hence ending up at Edgar Road.

'Alfie, he can't go out at the moment, can he, Salmon?' Rocky said.

'No, I heard the Barkers telling my owners that he's got to stay inside for a few weeks until he gets used to the place.'

'Right.' I felt words were going to choke me.

'So, what we're saying is that you've got a while to get used to the idea before you actually have to meet him,' Nellie said gently.

'OK.' This was the last thing I expected when I came out to see my friends. But now I had to go and tell George that another cat was living in his Tiger mum's house. But I had no idea how he'd react.

'It makes sense, Dad, I guess,' George said, I was amazed by his mature reaction. My boy constantly surprised me.

'Eh?' I expected him to react the way I had, feeling upset, angry maybe, at the idea of my Tiger being replaced.

'Dad, loneliness comes in all shapes and sizes, you taught me that. The Barkers have been very cat lonely without Tiger, and they have a good home. And the new cat, he probably lost his home so he must have been very lonely too. So, it makes sense that they have each other. After all it's a shame to let a good cat flap go to waste.'

'So, you don't feel that Tiger's been replaced?' He was so flippant about it.

'Don't be ridiculous, they will always love her in their hearts, like we do, but I know that they need this new cat too.'

'Right.' I wasn't sure I was following. 'But you said that I couldn't fall in love with another cat, because Tiger was irreplaceable.'

'Oh Dad, of course you can't replace her, but then cats are more intelligent than humans. Humans need us cats to survive, surely you understand that?'

'Um, yes, I guess I do.' I actually did hold with this logic. I'm not a vain cat, but we are superior to most animals and people, so George did have a point.

'It's like Pickles can't really be a cat, because he's a dog. It's the same for humans. I know this, it's part of my job to know this.'

Leaving me dumbfounded he made to go to the back door.

'I have to see Hana now, she's expecting me.'

Just what was happening to my little boy? And what was this job he kept talking about? It was driving me crazy not knowing, but that would have to wait, because now I had bigger fish to fry – if only – I had to wallow about the fact that there was another cat living in Tiger's house. Before too long I would have to meet him, and be nice to him, and not feel angry, hurt and incensed that he was not, and never would be, Tiger. I did understand the Barkers' need for a cat, I did understand Oliver's need for a home, but that was rational thought, my heart – which wasn't as rational – still hurt.

Chapter Sixteen

My confused state lasted all week, I was so upset. George would go out for long periods of time every single day and still refused to tell me where he was going. I did trust him – sort of anyway, but I worried. What if someone was taking advantage of him? What if he was putting himself in danger? I just didn't know what to do.

Polly was sitting with Pickles on her lap when I appeared from my morning constitutional, my best thinking time normally, but not today. Claire was pouring coffee for them both. Pickles was enjoying having his ears rubbed – that dog was seriously pampered, but he was so sweet and had grown on me at an alarming rate. When he first arrived, I worried that I would have to try hard to like him, what with him being a dog and all, but actually I took to him very quickly and he now felt like part of my family.

'I saw Marcus this morning and he said that Harold has perked right up,' Polly said.

'Really?'

'Yes, apparently an old friend has been to see him and it's cheered him up no end. Marcus said he's like a different man at the moment, although he still complains about everything, he is happier than usual and hasn't accused anyone of trying to kill him in days.'

'Do you think it's a woman?' Claire asked.

'Oh goodness, with his heart problem, I sincerely hope not,' Polly laughed. 'Marcus didn't say who it was, just that

his old friend is visiting every day, and somehow before official visiting time. He wondered if it was someone from that
group he goes to, you know the old people's group.'

'The Senior Centre? As long as he's happy it doesn't matter,'
Claire said. 'You know I've started talking to more people
on his ward. It's so sad, some of the old people in hospital
never get visitors.'

'That's so sad,' Polly said. 'If I get old I hope my children
visit me.'

'Polly, that's not something to be thinking about now.
Right, I said I'd bake Harold a cake to share around the ward
today, so I better get started.'

'But, Claire, you don't bake.'

'I know, but it's just a sponge cake, how hard can that be?'

Polly shook her head but then she had to leave to go to
work.

Turns out it's harder than Claire thought. Firstly she
managed to get flour all over the floor, and Pickles, who was
hoping to get some stray food, turned white and had to be
brushed off. Then she got eggshell in the eggs, and it took
ages to pick it out. When it finally came out of the oven it
looked terrible, all sunken and not anything like a cake should
look. The kitchen looked like a bombsite. Luckily I'd had
the foresight to watch from a safe distance.

'Right, I'm going to buy a cake,' Claire declared and went
out, leaving Pickles and me alone. There were a lot of places I
wanted to go to, the recreation ground, next door to see Hana
and question her about George, and part of me wanted to go
to Tiger's old house to see if I could catch a glimpse of the
new cat, but I couldn't go anywhere, not for a while anyway.

'Garden?' I asked Pickles. It was pretty cold but at least it wasn't raining and I needed some fresh air.

'Yes, please.' I went through the cat flap and waited. After a few seconds a tiny head appeared. Pickles' head. But his body didn't follow.

'What are you doing?' I asked. 'Come out, hurry up.'

'I can't seem to move,' he said, looking a little stricken.

'What do you mean you can't move?' I asked.

'I seem to be stuck,' he said, as he tried to wriggle. Oh, no, this was not what I needed. Pickles had finally done it, he'd become too big for the cat flap. What on earth was I supposed to do now?

I started circling around, trying to think.

'What are you doing?' Pickles asked.

'Thinking,' I replied. There was no way I could pull him from the front, I was a cat after all. And he was blocking the only way for me to get inside the house, so I was stuck outside. I sat down and started licking my paws.

'What are you doing?' Pickles asked again.

'Thinking,' I replied. I watched him try to heave himself out but he wasn't going anywhere as his paws swung up and down in the air. He'd be exhausted in no time at this rate.

'Have you finished thinking yet?' he asked.

'The thing is, Pickles, we are in a bit of a predicament,' I said.

'What's that?'

'You're stuck in a cat flap. You remember not long ago you were small but now you've grown. You're actually bigger than George, so you can't use our cat flap anymore.'

'OK, but how do I get out?' He looked panicked as his face scrunched up even more than normal.

'I'm afraid there's only one way, we have to wait for Claire to come back from the shops.'

'But how long will she be? This isn't comfortable, or even fun anymore.'

'She won't be long, but, Pickles, if you stop wriggling, and panicking then you'll be more comfortable,' I suggested. He did.

'Can we play a game while we wait?' he asked.

'Sure what do you want to play?'

'We could play I spy.'

He had learnt about I spy from the children, but couldn't really grasp the alphabet. Dogs.

'You go first,' I suggested.

'I spy with my little eye, something beginning with bird.'

'Bird,' I guessed.

'You are so good at this. Your turn, Alfie.'

I was beginning to despair when I heard Claire arrive home. I thought about waiting for her by the front doorstep but then I was worried that if I left him alone, Pickles would panic even more and hurt himself.

'Oh my goodness,' I heard Claire shout, and of course we both knew that we'd been saved. Claire must have seen Pickles' back end in the cat flap. What a sight to come home to.

'Right,' I heard her say. 'Pickles, stay still, I am going to gently pull you backwards.' I heard a little bit of huffing from Claire, before Pickles' face began to disappear backwards. Once he was freed I quickly went through the cat flap to join him.

'Well this is a bit of a pickle, Pickles.' Claire laughed at her own joke. 'You are going to have to stay inside now until one of us is here to let you out. And, Alfie, you and George will have to bear that in mind, and not rush out, because, Alfie, he might follow you and get stuck again.'

'Meow.' It wasn't ideal. This puppy had curtailed my freedom quite a lot so far and although I enjoyed his company, I valued my freedom. I wasn't sure I was happy not to be able to go outside.

'Or we could get a dog door, which is just like a bigger cat flap.' Her brows knotted as if she was thinking. 'Or you could do what Polly said and lose some weight, Pickles,' she finished, before she went to unpack her shopping.

'What are we going to do?' Pickles asked me wide-eyed.

'I am going to have some lunch,' I replied. 'And if you want your lunch too, let's hope Claire decides to go for the bigger door option.'

Chapter
Seventeen

Chapter
seventeen

I went to see my cat friends while I could still come and go of my own free will.

'Have any of you seen George?' I asked Nellie and Rocky. Elvis wasn't there.

'No, Alfie, I've barely seen him the past few days, but then we haven't seen much of you either.'

'I've been puppy-sitting, it's very time-consuming. But George has been going out and he's been gone quite a long time. I'm a bit worried.'

'I have no idea where he could be. As Rocky said, we've haven't seen him for a few days. I miss him of course,' Nellie said, sweetly. 'But do you think it's anything to do with the Barkers' new cat?'

'Actually, I seemed to be more upset about that than he was. He said the Barkers were lonely and of course they needed a cat. Part of me feels that I should trust him. The other part . . .'

'What does the other part say, Alfie?' Rocky asked.

'That I need to know what's going on, because it's the only way I can be sure he is safe.'

'Which part is going to win?' Nellie asked.

'Which do you think?' I raised my whiskers, we all knew what was happening.

I was going to have to follow George, just for my own peace of mind. Forget him and Hana now I needed to know more about where he went. But I really had to figure out how to do it so he didn't know, because George got incredibly cross with me when I did follow him once. And he hated the idea that I didn't trust him. I needed to think and I needed a plan. Luckily coming up with plans was one of the things I always did best.

'You know, you could ask Hana,' Rocky suggested, which made me want to kick myself if that was even possible, because I couldn't believe I hadn't thought of that already.

'Look, Alfie, I don't blame you for needing to know, in fact we'd all feel better if we knew George wasn't going to be in any trouble. After all we all love the lad,' Rocky said.

'Yes, you're right.'

'So if you need us to help in any way, then just let us know,' Nellie finished.

'Thanks, guys, I can always rely on you,' I said which reassured me. 'But you're right first I'll go and ask Hana.'

I knew I had to walk back home past the Barkers' house, and I still felt conflicted. As I approached, the new cat, Oliver, was sat on the windowsill, in the same spot Tiger used to sit. I felt my heart ache as I looked at him. He was black and white, a fine-looking feline. He also looked very intelligent. And, of course, nothing like Tiger. He looked up just as I was staring at him and I felt embarrassed, but I raised my whiskers in as friendly a way as I could muster. He raised his whiskers back. He clearly wasn't a young cat, but he needed a home, and goodness knows enough cats were looking for good homes. The Barkers had a good home and they needed a cat because, as George said, they didn't feel right without one. So I had to come to terms with this because what was important was that this cat had a loving home now. It's exactly what my Tiger would have wanted.

With thoughts of Tiger in my head, I went to Hana's house, and let myself in through her cat flap. I didn't normally go to her house alone, because she was George's friend, but needs must.

'Hi,' I said as alerted by the noise of the cat flap she approached.

'Alfie, this is a surprise,' she said. She really was the sweetest cat.

'How are you?' I asked. I wished Hana would come out more but she liked to be at home. It takes all sorts of cats to make a world.

'I'm good, thanks, we're quite busy here, what with Harold being in hospital, there's a lot going on,' she said. 'But I think he's going to be alright. You know humans though, I just try to be a good cat and listen to them all.'

'I guess it's a bit stressful for you, though, Hana.'

'I just worry about my humans. and I just wish Harold would come home and things could get back to normal.'

'Of course you do. And George told me that Harold had to be in a bit longer,' I started. 'Talking of George, I don't want you to betray a confidence or anything but I just want to know he's safe and I don't know where he's going every day.'

Hana tilted her head to one side.

'You know he said he bet you were going to come and ask me.'

Oh no, I'm obviously predictable.

'I'm sorry but you know I do worry about him.'

'I know you do, but, Alfie, George said he has a job. It keeps him busy, but he said he can't tell me. Although I think he only doesn't want to tell me in case I tell you!' She grinned. She had a kind smile.

'You can't get anything past that boy,' I said, grinning back. 'Hana, I don't want you to think I'm a terrible dad but I just want to know he's safe.'

'I know, it's like Sylvie and Connie. But actually I think Sylvie might be worse than you.'

'Thank you, I think.'

'Alfie, I know George is a bit mysterious, but he is smart and if he says that he's safe, I think you should believe him. I know it's hard not knowing but George taught me a saying, "curiosity kills a cat".'

I didn't think that was the exact saying, because I was incredibly curious and I was definitely alive.

'Hana, I won't ask you to lie to George for me . . .' I also knew he'd be really cross if he found out I'd been trying to get information from his friend.

'Thank you, Alfie, I won't lie to him, but if he doesn't ask me then I don't need to tell him.' She blinked at me.

'But while I'm here, you wouldn't care to shed light on the relationship between you and George would you?' I asked.

'He said you would probably ask me about that too.' She grinned. 'So, maybe you should ask George.'

'You are a star, Hana, and thank you again.' She was right, I should ask my son. Not that he would ever tell me.

I chatted to her for a bit longer and then I said goodbye. Now I had to come up with another way to find out what George was doing and where he was going.

George was going out early in the morning at the moment, and we didn't see him again until the afternoon. Once I had a clear idea of his schedule I could put the next part of my plan into action, to follow him to wherever he was going. I would need to remain unseen, and he would be none the wiser. It was foolproof.

As I've said, I have had many plans in the past, and on the whole they have worked out. They may have included a few dangerous incidents but I'm still here to tell the tale. But this plan, with George, was crucial to get right. When I saw him later that day, I gave him one last chance to tell me where he'd been going.

'It's my job, Dad, I've told you a million times.'

I was pretty sure he hadn't told me even half of that many times, actually.

'OK, but you know as your dad I would love to know more about it. You know where it is, and what you do.'

'I can't tell you. It's a secret. You remember when Tommy decided he was going to be a spy?'

'Oh yes, I vaguely remember that, it was a few years back now wasn't it?'

'Yes, and he said he was going to be a spy and catch bad people but he wouldn't be able to tell anyone that was his job.'

'Are you trying to tell me you're a spy?' I asked, horrified. When Tommy described it, it sounded like a dangerous job. I felt panic in my fur, I was pretty sure cats didn't get to be spies but then what did I know?

'Of course I'm not a spy, I don't actually even know what one is,' George replied, laughing at me. He was infuriating.

'It was just an example because my job is a secret, but it's not dangerous and you just need to trust me.'

'I do trust you but I really don't understand why you can't tell me anything.'

'I can tell you that what I do is very important.'

It was time for me to put my plan into action.

The following day, I let George leave, and snuck out quickly behind him. The weather was closing in, the clocks were about to change, which meant we would have more hours of darkness than this cat cared for, but never mind. Winter wasn't my favourite season, although thankfully it included Christmas – its only redeeming quality. Anyway, I followed George out of the cat flap and to the front of the house. Keeping out of sight I watched him walk past Hana's house and I set off behind him, keeping a safe distance. He crossed a road, but I got delayed by traffic and he got more of a head start as I hurried after him. I realised we were relatively near the children's school but instead of turning towards it he turned the other way. He strode confidently, this was clearly somewhere that George had been a number of times before. He turned around a couple of times but I hid either behind a pedestrian or in a hedge and felt pretty confident about my journey. Finally he came to a stop, but I hadn't caught up with him. From where I stood, he looked to be in some kind of queue with humans. I was confused until I saw there was a big red bus parked by the queue. Surely not? Before I could move, I spotted George, weaving himself between people's legs and hopping onto the bus. I tried to follow him but was blocked by a woman and a pram, who was struggling to get on. When she finally did the doors closed, and I was left standing on the street, watching, helplessly, the bus pull away with my kitten on it.

As I walked home, I felt as if I had failed and tried to nurse my despair. George clearly had been on the bus before but how? Why? And had no one noticed, because as far as I was aware, cats didn't get to travel on buses. He was sneaking on the bus, and what's more he was getting away with it. Although I hadn't managed to get as far as I would have liked, I conceded that at least now I had more information and information is power. Or at least something I could use to plan my next step.

I had to figure out a way of getting on the bus without George noticing, and stay hidden on the bus, until it was time for him to get off. I had even more questions than answers at this point which only fuelled my determination to crack this mystery once and for all.

The following day, my determination increased. I rose early, cleaned myself, and waited downstairs for George to emerge. After what felt like ages, he padded downstairs with Toby and Summer. Claire and Jonathan followed after, and as the noise of the morning began to fill the house. I managed to pull George away before we tucked into our breakfast.

'I wanted to catch you before you went to work,' I said. 'Just to check that you're alright.'

'I'm fine, Dad, but I'm not going to work today.'

What? So much for my carefully constructed plan and early morning start.

'You're not?' I tried to sound nonchalant about it, after all I didn't need him to feel suspicious.

'No, Dad, no one works all the time, even Jonathan has time off every week.'

'Well that's true, but of course as I don't know about your job, I have no idea what your working arrangements are.' Again I tried to feign disinterest. I looked at my paw.

'Ah, well I have a day off today and I thought what better way to spend it than with my dad. And as it's the weekend, we might not have to babysit Pickles, so maybe we can go out and spend some time together?' he asked me, hopefully.

'I'd love to,' I replied, feeling a little emotional. 'Actually, George, I've missed you.'

'And I've missed you too, Dad. Come on let's not waste any time, and make the most of the day.'

I couldn't think of anything I would rather do. Even if it did mean that my plan to discover George's job would have to wait.

Chapter
Eighteen

We'd spent most of the weekend together, been to see Dustbin, caught up with our friends on Edgar Road, hung out with Hana. It was like old times. But the saying curiosity killed the cat was actually proving to be apt, because I felt as if I was dying to know about George's job.

I repeated my steps of the last time I tried to follow George. I was up at the crack of dawn, but then so were Claire and Jonathan.

'Oh, Alfie, you're up early,' Claire said fussing me as Jonathan made coffee. I wasn't sure what was going on.

'I'm hopeful that I'll get my team finalised today,' Jonathan said, handing Claire a mug.

'I really hope so, Jon, this is getting to all of us now.'

'I know, darling and I am sorry but it's just—'

'I know, temporary. And I do understand but I think now it really is enough. You know Toby was so upset last night because he has a big science project coming up. He held it back from you because he was worried you'd be too busy.'

'That makes me very sad, Claire.' Jonathan sounded upset. 'And when I get back from work tonight, I will talk to him about it, I promise. And I'll make time to help him in any way I can.'

'I'd quite like to spend some time with you too. This weekend you've been glued to your laptop, Jon.'

'I know, and I'm sorry but I had to finalise all the reports for today, it will get better. It has to get better.' His voice sounded sad.

We all tried so hard to believe his words but we'd heard them before. I didn't have time to dwell on that as the children and George descended. George and I had already established that he was going to work today, so I was ready. I was more than ready.

We were interrupted by a surprise ring on the doorbell, who would be popping by before breakfast? Our morning routine was underway; the children at the table waiting for their cereal and toast, Jonathan upstairs getting ready to leave for work. As Claire opened the door, there stood Matt on the doorstep holding Pickles. I hadn't accounted for this.

'Thanks so much, Claire. Polly was up at the crack of dawn to get the train to Manchester and I've got an early meeting.' He handed a squirming Pickles to Claire.

'No worries, we're all up early anyway,' she said kindly. As Matt left, Claire shut the door behind her and put Pickles down, releasing his lead. As Pickles shuffled into the kitchen, I tried to catch him on his own.

'Pickles, I have to tell you that I'm going out this morning, on urgent cat business, with George.' It wasn't strictly accurate but I needed to keep it simple for him. 'So you need to stay here, and I'll be back later.' In reality I had no idea where I was going, so I certainly had no idea when I'd be back.

'OK, Alfie,' he said and took up his position under the table to catch the children's scraps. Great, crisis averted – I went to watch George leave.

I tried not to act as if I was watching George's every move, while watching his every move. No sooner had Claire rushed the children out of the house for school, George headed out. I waited a beat and went out after him.

I went through the back garden and was about to squeeze under the gate, which had been left open. I started bounding down the street after him, he wasn't too far in front of me, and was just about the cross the road when I heard a voice behind me.

'Wait for me.' Oh no, it was Pickles. He caught up with me.

'I told you to wait at home.' I cursed the fact they had put a bigger cat flap – which they said was a doggy door – in at home and double cursed the fact the gate was open, because there was no way he would have got out of the garden otherwise.

'Where's the fun in that?' he asked. 'I wanted to go on urgent cat business.'

Yet again I had a decision to make, and no time in which to think about it. I could take Pickles home which would be the sensible option, or I could continue to follow George and hope for the best. I wanted more than anything to find out where George was going and if I went back home now, who knew when I'd get the chance again. Especially if Pickles was always going to follow me. No, I needed to make sure George was safe, that was the most important thing. Pickles would have to come with me, but I definitely wouldn't let him cross any roads on his own.

'Stay close to me and try not to be seen,' I said. This was not part of my plan.

'Why?'

'We're planning a surprise for George, so he can't know we're here yet.'

'Oh fun!'

I shook my tail. This was anything but fun.

Tentatively I led Pickles safely across the road and followed George to the bus stop.

'Right, come on, we have to get on the bus but no one can see us.'

We managed to get on by staying close to some human legs and then as I saw George making his way up the back of the bus, I quickly got Pickles to come with me and we hid behind a big shopping trolley at the front.

'Be really quiet and still,' I commanded as Pickles wiggled his bottom excitedly. I could see how George got away with it – although I was unsure how on earth he'd learnt to take the bus in the first place. Most people were staring at their phones, a couple had books, so it was relatively easy to go unnoticed. When the bus stopped, Pickles and I lurched a bit, so I sort of snuggled into him to try to keep us still. At the next stop someone stood on my tail as they were getting off. I had to bite my tongue not to yelp although it hurt. After what felt like ages, I noticed George go and wait by the doors, and I told Pickles to prepare to get off the bus. I mentally crossed my paws that he would stay close to me, I couldn't imagine the sort of trouble we'd be in if I lost him on a bus. The bus came to an abrupt halt, and George, looking every inch the expert, hopped off. We followed managing once again to fall into step with some humans. I have to say, as the wind hit my face I felt relieved that that part of our journey was over. I was partly impressed with my kitten, that he had managed to figure this bus thing out, and part worried if he did this every day. We were lucky that he hadn't been hurt by a human standing on him, or worse. I had found the bus ride very stressful, although that could have been down to the fact I was trying so hard to keep Pickles in line.

'What now?' Pickles asked. He was very excited, whereas I was worried now. We were far from home, and Pickles really shouldn't be with me. George and I shouldn't be this far from home, let alone the puppy.

'Come on, we best not lose George now,' I said, beckoning him. We followed George at a safe distance, and after a short while we came upon a large, modern building. I finally figured out where we were as the penny dropped. The vehicles parked outside were the same as the ones which had come to collect Harold when he was ill the first time. An ambulance. George had brought us to the hospital. And he seemed to think he worked here.

Confused, I ran up to the door just as he walked through. It was an automatic door, so it opened and I strode through, although there were a few people around, no one seemed to notice either George or myself. The door shut and I saw Pickles standing on the other side. Desperate not to lose George, or Pickles, I stood close to the door which opened again.

'Hurry up,' I said.

'Woof woof, woof,' Pickles replied. I saw George stop, after all us cats have excellent hearing, much better than humans. He froze for a second, as the door closed again then turned around and saw us. I braced myself as he approached me; he did not look happy.

'What on earth are you doing here?' he hissed. Just then

the door opened and some humans walked in, Pickles happily trotted in behind them.

'Um, we thought we would come and see Harold?' I tried.

'No, no you didn't. You followed me because you couldn't trust me about my job and now you're probably going to ruin everything,' he carried, on, ushering us to a doorway where hopefully no one would see us.

'Wo—' Pickles started, wiggling his bottom excitedly.

'No Pickles,' I hissed. 'We need to be really quiet.

'George, I admit I needed to see where you've been going, I was worried sick. And I've been trying to follow you for a while but today was the first day I actually got it right, only I got it wrong because Pickles followed, and I am sorry but I just love you so much and need to know you're safe.'

'Look, you've got what you came here for, you know where I work. Yes I work in a hospital, yes Harold is here and my job is to make people happy and not just Harold. It's really important to me and if you've ruined it, I will never forgive you.'

I felt awful, I should have trusted him, but I also needed, as a parent, to know where he was going. If only he'd told me. No, actually if he told me he was doing this I would have still worried and had to follow him anyway.

'George,' I said, in my best parental authoritative voice. 'I am your father and I do trust you but you have undertaken a very treacherous journey, and anything could have happened. I was worried sick about you, what if you'd been run over, or stepped on, or the bus driver caught you? Anything could have happened did you even think about that?'

'None of that did happen though, did it? Look, Dad, I

know you worry but I did this very carefully. The first time I came with Marcus.'

'Marcus brought you?' I asked with surprise.

'Not exactly. I knew he was visiting Harold so I followed him, and I learnt the whole layout, then I started coming on my own, in the mornings mostly when I knew they didn't have visitors.'

'Why couldn't you tell me all this?'

'Harold said it had to be a secret or I wouldn't be able to come anymore.'

'I think he meant from humans. What now?' I asked, as I noticed Pickles had become bored and restless.

'You and Pickles go home and I'll go and visit Harold.'

'Um.' I hadn't quite thought through this part of my plan.

'What?' George asked.

'I'm not sure how to get home. You see I was so busy watching you, and making sure Pickles was alright I didn't pay that much attention to the route.'

'OK, then how about you and Pickles wait here, stay hidden and I'll go and visit my friends.'

'Friends? I thought it was Harold.'

'Dad, there are lots of lonely people on his ward who like to see me. That's my job, I visit lonely people and cheer them up.'

'Wow, I am so proud of you.' I felt emotional.

'Yes, but you're stopping me from doing my job.'

'Could we come and watch you, just this once?' I asked.

'No, absolutely not, there's no way that I am going to let you come with me.'

'OK.' I resigned myself to stay hidden, and try to keep

Pickles under control – goodness knows how I was going to do that. As George walked off, Pickles made a break for it and ran after him. I had no choice but to follow.

George made his way to a back stairwell where we joined him.

'What?' he asked.

'It was Pickles,' I replied truthfully.

'It really was,' Pickles said. 'I am trying to be a cat so I need to cheer people up too. After all this is important cat business.'

I raised my whiskers at George, he had put the cat idea into Pickles' head after all. George hid us round a corner until someone pushed the door open and came out from the stairwell, he hissed at us to be quick and thankfully we made it safely in just before the door closed.

'There's a lift,' he explained, 'but I can't reach the buttons so this way I know exactly what floor to go to.'

'You've really put a lot of work into this haven't you?' I said, impressed.

'Of course, it's my job as I try to keep telling you,' he replied. 'You don't just sail into a job this important, you know, it takes a lot of thought and talent.'

That told me. We walked up two flights of stairs, Pickles was huffing and puffing, the dog was really unfit – compared to us anyway. When we were on the right floor, according to George, there was a wedge keeping it open.

'Harold arranged for whichever patient is allowed out of bed, to go for a little walk, and wedge this door open, he does it every day,' George explained. 'The first time I came along I got stuck here for ages waiting for someone to come through, so we don't take any chances now.'

He squeezed through the door, and then looked at Pickles.

'Dad, if you come through we can push it open further for Pickles.' I was beginning to think my son was some kind of genius.

It took a bit of effort but finally we were all through the door.

'Right, this is the last bit,' George told us. 'The door is shut but people go in and out all the time, so what we must do is wait around the side, and as soon as the door opens we run for it. Whoever gets there first can hold the door open for Pickles,' George said.

'What if I get there first?' Pickles asked. George just shook his tail. I wondered how long he would remain angry at me for.

We huddled behind a pillar and, as George predicted, someone came through and opened the door. We were about to make a run for it, but when we turned around to tell Pickles to run, we saw him running faster than we've ever seen him in the opposite direction.

Chapter Nineteen

'Quick,' George said, as we both sprinted as fast as we could after Pickles. He was about to enter another ward, as he chased behind a man pushing a child in a wheel-chair. We caught up with him and just made it through another door before it banged aggressively behind us, I only just managed to whip my tail through in time. As we caught our breath, I looked around and saw that we were in a bright-coloured place. The man carried on pushing the chair, somehow Pickles had hitched a lift. I looked at George in horror. Pickles was sitting on the lap of the little girl in the wheelchair, but thankfully she had hidden him under her dressing gown so the man hadn't noticed. She was smiling and we followed them until she was pushed to a bed. I had a bad feeling.

'This must be the children's ward,' George said.

So this was a hospital ward I thought, as I saw a row of beds with children and a few adults next to them. I looked at George.

'This is not good is it?' I asked.

'No, Dad. If we get caught there will be a whole heap of trouble.' And as if to prove the point, Pickles jumped down from the girl's lap and started sliding around the floor.

'Look, it's a dog,' one of the children shouted, as those who were able got out of bed and crowded around Pickles. The adults looked at each other uneasily. As did George and I who were trying to stay unnoticed behind a curtain.

'Should he be here?' one of them asked.

'I don't think so, shall I go and get the ward sister?' another replied.

'Can't we play with him?' the boy who was stroking him asked. 'Please, he's so cute.'

'Woof,' Pickles agreed.

'We don't know anything about him,' the adult with him replied. 'But he shouldn't be here, I'm sure.'

'Maybe he's one of those dogs who can visit hospitals,' another adult suggested. 'I've read about them.'

'Maybe, but shouldn't he have an adult with him and be on a lead? What if he bites a child?' the woman who said she would go and get sister asked, before she left the ward.

'Oh no,' I said. Yet again, I realised I should have taken Pickles home, I shouldn't have come, I should have waited, I should have trusted George. So many things were going wrong and I had a bad feeling in my fur. This was not one of my finer plans. 'If they catch him, what will they do?'

'I don't know but Harold says to me it's imperative that I don't get caught, which is why I keep it so quiet. He says there will be big trouble if I'm found out.'

We were already in big trouble, that much was clear and we couldn't get to Pickles without being seen. I wracked my brain for answers, but I couldn't come up with a great deal of options.

'Do you think we should stay hidden and wait and see what happens?' I asked.

'I don't see we have much choice. Oh boy, Dad, why did you have to come with him today?'

I asked myself the same thing.

'Right what is going on,' a voice boomed and a large woman who seemed almost like a giant compared to most of the children, and us of course, loomed. The children, who didn't seem very happy to see her, parted and I could see her staring at Pickles, who was wagging his bottom at her excitedly. I wanted to rush in and save him but I didn't know how. A shadow appeared on the floor as she reached out and picked him up. He licked her face.

'Uggh, you dirty thing, you cannot be on a ward with ill children,' she shrieked. Poor Pickles looked confused. After all everyone he encountered fell for his charm, so I did feel a bit bad for him. He tried to wriggle out of her arms as she tightened her grip. How would I ever make this up to George?

'Has he got a collar on?' one of the parents asked, but I knew he didn't. Polly had said she'd had him chipped, but decided against a collar. Knowing Pickles he'd have only eaten it.

'No, but then he's probably chipped,' another voice said, which was a relief.

'Well I don't have time for this. I'll call the dog warden and they can deal with it,' the woman said. I felt my heart sink. I didn't know what a dog warden was but what if they took Pickles somewhere and we never saw him again? What if the dog warden was as mean as the woman who held a Pickles in her arms?

'Dad, we have to do something,' George hissed.

'Right,' I said, another plan leapt into my head. 'We will have to follow that woman, with Pickles, and whatever we do we can't let him out of our sight.'

'Good idea,' George said, and I began to feel a bit like the adult again. So far, George had proved himself mature and sensible. Perhaps he wasn't technically supposed to come to the hospital but he was coming for the right reasons, and I had somehow messed that up for him, which didn't make me the best father in the world. As well as getting Pickles out of here, I would have to put that right. It's what parents did when we screwed up. After all, we were only cats at the end of the day.

The woman marched out of the ward, leaving children crying in her wake but we couldn't afford to dwell on that. George and I raised our whiskers at each other in understanding and followed her, ever careful not to be seen we dodged behind trolleys along the corridor. We watched her march into an office, and put Pickles down on a chair.

'Stay there,' she commanded. Even Pickles looked terrified of her, with her stern voice I couldn't blame him, but Pickles was sitting stiller than I'd ever seen him.

Thankfully, she hadn't shut the door but we didn't dare being seen yet. I poked my head around.

'How on earth did you get into my ward?' she asked.

'Woof,' Pickles replied.

'Well I won't have it. I run a tight ship and there is no room for dogs.' She narrowed her eyes at him, and Pickles trembled.

'Right.' She typed something into the computer, and then picked up a phone. I could barely breathe as I watched it unfold. 'Hello, yes I'm calling from the hospital, and there's a dog running around here, totally out of control.'

There was a pause.

'I don't know if he's dangerous,' she continued. I glanced at George, Pickles was possibly the least dangerous dog in the world.

Another pause.

'No, he's not foaming at the mouth. Listen, I need someone to come up and get him out of the hospital. Out of the children's ward.'

Another pause.

'Make sure you hurry, thank you.'

The phone went dead.

What was going to happen? They were on the way to get him and we had no way of getting him out of the room without being seen.

'Sister, Sister, there's a problem in bay three.' A nurse came running in. Thankfully she didn't notice as I tucked myself into the corner of the office. Sister looked the nurse, then at Pickles.

'Stay,' she commanded and ran out. She pulled the door shut behind her, but George managed to get his paw in before it closed totally. We were all back together, thankfully but that wasn't necessarily the end of our problems as we had to figure out a way to get out of here.

'Pickles,' I hissed, 'come with me.'

Pickles wiggled his bottom, but thankfully hopped off the chair.

'This is so much fun,' he said. I had no words. 'Apart from the scary woman. I didn't much like the scary woman.'

'Look,' George said as we began to make our way out of the ward and hopefully to safety, gesturing with his whiskers. 'It's a laundry cart, I've seen them before, they might take us to Harold's ward if we're lucky.' He gestured with his paw to a big cart, which had high sides, there was no way Pickles could jump up to it. Perhaps Pickles might be able to fit in at the side?

'Pickles, do exactly as I say,' I commanded in my sternest voice.

'I always do,' Pickles replied. He really, really didn't. We approached the cart. There was a man with one hand on it and he was talking to someone else. Thankfully he had his back to us.

'Right,' I said, holding open the slit with a paw, 'jump in.'

'Are you coming?' Pickles asked.

'I'm right behind you.' Pickles started to climb in and, although his bottom got caught up a bit, I gave him a shove with my paw and he was in. I followed, as did George.

'Yuk, it stinks,' Pickles said. It wasn't the most pleasant smell, but then it was a laundry cart. And thankfully it wasn't too full. And this was his fault so if anyone had a right to complain . . .

'It's better than the dog warden,' George hissed at him. He wasn't delighted; we were still in big trouble with him.

'Where are you going now?' I heard a human voice say from outside the cart.

'To Carpenter ward,' he replied.

'That's Harold's ward,' George whispered, flooded with relief.

'Pickles,' I warned, 'from now on you do exactly what we say and you follow us. No going off on your own or getting any bright ideas.'

'OK.' he replied. I didn't feel full of confidence but surely the worst had happened and we'd escaped, so that should be alright and at least now we were going to see Harold. I just had to make everything else up to George, that was all.

We were on the move. I felt the trolley being pushed forward. There was a bit of a shunt as we went through the door, but I motioned for Pickles to stay quiet. Another shunt told us we were through more doors and then the cart stopped.

'Let me check,' George said, quietly, looking out of the gap. 'Yay, we're here,' he said, sounding happier than he had since we'd arrived. 'Right, follow me. I am the expert here, so it might be an idea to remember that.'

I would never forget that again. George went first, Pickles next and I brought up the rear so I could keep an eye on Pickles. We sort of herded him, it was the only way. Without further incident, we managed to get to another room similar the children's ward. Then, in the bed nearest the door, sat up in his striped pyjamas, was Harold. I was so pleased to see him, I nearly yowled, I realised how much I'd missed him. George jumped up onto the bed.

'I wondered where you'd got to, you're late today,' Harold said, but he stroked George, and nuzzled him. 'I was worried, that's all,' he added.

'Meow,' George said. Then he looked down at us, and Harold did the same.

'Oh my, how on earth did you get these two in here?' he asked.

'Meow,' I said.

'Hold on,' Harold said. He put George onto his bed, and slowly swung his legs around. Then, holding onto the bed frame, he bent down and picked Pickles up. I jumped onto his bed when he was back in it, and the three of us crowded him.

'Well I never,' another old man said, getting off the bed he was in and coming over.

'I have no idea how they all got here,' Harold said. 'I mean George's pretty clever, as is Alfie, but how did they manage to sneak a dog in here?'

The other man chuckled. 'It's amazing isn't it. Can I show him around?' He picked Pickles up. Pickles licked his face.

'Yes but don't get caught mind. If a member of staff appears you have to hide. George, sorry I know you know this already, but Alfie and Pickles, it's important.'

'Meow.' I had already gathered as much.

Arthur, the elderly patient, took Pickles around the ward to see other patients, and they all cheered up immediately.

'Dad, I know that you worry about me but alongside Harold I visit other people here, so would you stay here while I do my rounds?' he asked.

'You are careful, aren't you?' I replied, our heads were touching. Harold looked around for his glasses, which were on the top of his head.

'I've never been caught,' George replied giving me a withering look. 'Unlike some.'

'Sorry, sorry,' I whispered.

'Yowl,' he said to Harold, giving him a nuzzle.

'Right you are, boy, see you in a minute.' Harold obviously knew the drill by now and I couldn't help but feel proud of my son. He had an important role here.

'George is like a tonic here,' he said. 'People love him

coming here, and he cheers us all up no end. You should be very proud.'

The mews choked in my throat, but I still felt guilty for the fact I had followed him here.

'Some people are so lonely, when my family, well our family comes to visit I always send them to talk to some of those who never have visitors. See Neville, in the corner?' I looked at a man who seemed very white but then Arthur approached with Pickles and a big smile appeared on his face. I felt like yowling, it was bittersweet. These people weren't well and they were lonely, some of them, and that wasn't right.

'Meow?' What can we do? I asked.

'It's terrible, not knowing what to do.' But what on earth could we do about it?

'Incoming,' Harold said, and tucked me under his bed sheet. Arthur hid Pickles under the bed he was next to.

'Right, gentlemen,' a nurse, who wasn't as severe as the sister, said. She had a kind voice from what I could hear, I obviously couldn't see her. 'About to bring your medicine, is everyone alright?'

'Yes, thanks,' they chorused.

'Good, back in a mo,' she said.

'They always come round to tell us they're coming round, it's very strange,' Harold said. 'But the good thing is that we know the medicine is coming, so we know to keep you all hidden. Can't have you getting caught now, can we?' Not after last time.

It was so much fun. I did feel bad for the men on the ward, they clearly weren't at their best, but there was a nice atmosphere. Even Harold laughed a couple of times.

'Right,' he said, after the medicine had been given out, 'someone will have to get George because it's visiting time soon and the family will be here – you need to get out before they come.' Some of the people, the more mobile ones, from the ward had gathered at Harold's bed and Pickles and I were both there now.

'I'll get him,' a man offered.

'Only because you want to see your fancy woman, Giles,' Arthur said and they all laughed.

Giles returned with George hidden in his dressing gown and we looked on from Harold's bed.

'It's been so grand to see you all,' Harold said, he sounded emotional. 'I do miss you, but I'll be home soon. And you guys better get ready to go now.'

'Meow,' George said.

'Incoming,' Arthur shouted and we all, having learned the drill, hid under the sheet. I looked at Pickles.

'Stay still,' I said, he was wiggling his tail like mad.

'I am,' he said. He was not.

'Pickles, you'll get caught again,' George warned.

'I will not,' he said defiantly. 'I'm a good cat.'

He really wasn't either.

'What is this?' a voice said. Thankfully it didn't sound like the woman from the children's ward, but George and I stayed still as statues. However, Pickles was still wiggling. Oh no. I had a bad feeling. Suddenly the sheet was pulled back, and exposed us all.

'That's a breach of my human rights,' Harold screeched. 'I could have been naked.'

'No, Harold, you couldn't,' a man's voice said, although he

sounded kind. 'You wear your pyjamas in here, but more to the point why are there two cats and a pug in your bed?' I thought I saw his lips twitch. A woman in a nurse's uniform joined him to see what was going on.

'Well I never,' she said.

'They're just visiting,' Harold said, but he did sound contrite.

'How on earth did two cats and a puppy get in here?' The male nurse scratched his head.

'And what do we do now? Should we call the dog warden?' the female nurse said.

'You can't call the dog warden for cats,' Harold said, to my relief. 'And anyway, I happen to know them.'

'You know them?' the male nurse asked.

'Yes, they live on my street. My Marcus will be here any minute now, surely he can arrange for them to be taken home.'

George gave me another scowl. We were going to be in big trouble when our humans heard about this but then, there was no way around it. We could make a run for it, but what if they caught us and called the dog warden? And what would the dog warden do with cats? Was there a cat warden? There were so many questions running around my head, I didn't notice Marcus approaching.

'Hello—' he said before he stopped short.

'Hey, son,' Harold said, innocently.

'What on earth is going on?' Poor Marcus's brows were etched in confusion.

'It seems,' the male nurse started to explain, 'that these three somehow came to visit, and I'm sure it will come as no surprise to you that animals are not supposed to be on hospital grounds.'

'Of course not, but how on earth did they get here?' We all looked at Marcus innocently, as did Harold now. Another staff member approached.

'I just spoke to Lisa in the children's ward and she said a dog was found there earlier. She didn't mention any cats though.'

'Have you been causing havoc?' Marcus asked. We all looked at him as if butter wouldn't melt.

'Meow,' I said as softly as I could.

'They've been cheering us all up no end, I can tell you,' Arthur said.

'Still, they shouldn't be here, so can you take them home?' The male nurse sounded kind but firm.

'Of course, although I don't have a lead or anything to put them in and I came by bus. Would you mind if I called a friend?'

'No, and while you do that, as long as you take full responsibility that they don't go anywhere else in the hospital, they can stay here until someone can collect them.' He grinned and left us. I was more than a bit relieved.

'Dad, you should have phoned me, Claire must be worried sick about Pickles.'

Oh dear, we hadn't thought of that.

'You know I'm hopeless at using the mobile phone,' Harold grumbled. Marcus had pulled his out and called Claire.

'Claire, I'm at the hospital, but so are Alfie, George and Pickles,' he said.

I could hear Claire scream, but I couldn't make out the words.

'I know, I know, I had no idea but I've just arrived, can you come and get them?'

More noise came from the phone.

'Claire's on her way,' he said as he hung up. 'But she's not happy, and you guys are in big trouble. You too, Dad.'

Oh boy, I knew that I would be the one getting the blame for this, after all I was supposed to be the responsible adult. I don't think Harold counted as that, so it would all be on me.

We all felt sad to say our goodbyes. Claire walked into the ward, with a stern look on her face. She was wielding a lead for Pickles and our carrier as she rushed towards us. We all cowered slightly.

'It took me ages to park but I finally got a space,' Claire said. 'I've been worried sick, looking everywhere for Pickles and the cats, Jonathan got called out of a meeting as I phoned him in hysterics. He suggested they might be with Hana and as no one was home, I sort of hoped that was the case, but I was this close to calling Polly who would have been frantic as well.' The words gushed out of Claire and as I knew her so well I knew she was angry with us. With me.

'I know, I thought that as soon as I saw them. Shall I help you get them into the car?' Marcus asked.

'Please, that would be great. And, Harold, if you get any more unexpected visitors, perhaps you'd let me know,' she said, wagging her finger at him.

George wouldn't talk to me on the journey back to Edgar Road, I tried to apologise to him but he didn't want to hear it. When we got home, we were all led to the kitchen for our telling off.

'I am so angry,' Claire said. 'But, Alfie, you're the adult so I'm holding you responsible. What were you thinking? And how on earth did you get to the hospital? Anyway, I have to go to the supermarket before I pick the children up from school, I've wasted most of the day trying to find you. And before you even think about going out again I'm locking the cat flap.'

As she stormed off, it seemed we were all grounded.

Chapter
Twenty

Winter had settled in, and the frosty atmosphere in the house was even thicker than the frost outside. And, it was all my fault. Pickles couldn't be held responsible because he was a baby – however I was not. In the days following our hospital visit, George wasn't talking to me, he was going off to see Hana, but I knew he hadn't risked going back to the hospital, because he was never gone long enough. He was blaming me for the fact he had lost his job, and not only that but the people he cheered up in hospital were missing out. I felt as if I might drown with guilt.

Claire kept telling me off, I mean if I heard 'anything could have happened to Pickles and it would have been all your fault, Alfie,' one more time, then I would go mad.

Polly and Matt were upset when they were told, and Claire felt awful, when she spoke to them she blamed herself rather than me, but Polly said she couldn't be responsible for Pickles following George and I. Tomasz came round and fixed bolts to the gate, so it wouldn't blow open again. There were a lot of factors involved in Pickles following us to the hospital, but the upshot; I had well and truly messed up in so many ways.

When they weren't angry, they were all astounded about how we managed to get to the hospital. I couldn't tell them, of course, at least they didn't know George had been going for ages. Harold had kept that quiet from what I could tell. The only person, other than the children, who wasn't angry with me was Pickles. But then he had no idea why everyone was making such a fuss, he kept saying it was his best day ever. At least one of us was happy. I didn't have the heart to be cross with him, although I did tell him again that he mustn't try to get out with us.

I knew I had to come up with a plan to make it up to George. He avoided me at home, and he missed Harold. I tried to talk to him but he wouldn't have any of it. While Claire took Pickles and the children on the school run, I headed out to seek the advice of my friends. Because I had to put this right.

It was so cold outside, the wind was ruffling my fur as I made my way to our recreation space. I saw Nellie first, then Elvis and Rocky, but with them was Oliver, the Barkers' rescue cat. I stopped a short distance away and took a breath. I knew I would meet him at some point but I hadn't thought about that properly – not with everything going on. It looked as if the time was now. I braced myself and told myself that I could do this.

'Alfie,' Nellie said, coming up to me and giving me a nuzzle; as my friends greeted me they realised how hard this was for me. I was so grateful.

'Hi, everyone,' I said. Then I turned to the new cat. 'Hi, Oliver, I'm Alfie, I've seen you at the window, but welcome to Edgar Road.'

'Thanks, Alfie, I've heard all about you, from the Barkers as well as these guys.' He was warm in his greeting and I immediately liked him. I couldn't help but think of him in Tiger's bed, or in her garden, but didn't matter, not really.

'Really? The Barkers talk about me?'

'They told me about Tiger and how she had cat friends in the neighbourhood, and how you and George were her closest friends.'

'That's nice to hear,' I said, a little choked with emotion. 'So tell us about yourself?' I was determined to make an effort. It's what Tiger would have wanted.

'I love food in jelly, especially fish. I like to play and my favourite toy is a padded fish which I keep with me, and I love nothing more than to curl up in a good box. I had a best friend, Copper, and I miss him a bit. It's so nice to have friends here as I've been at the shelter a while. In fact, I couldn't be happier to have arrived here on Edgar Road – especially at my age.'

'How old are you, if you don't mind me asking?' I said.

'I'm twelve years old, Alfie, still a few lives left in me yet.'

'You've got plenty of friends here,' I said. Oliver grinned. He'd fit right in, I was a very good judge of cat.

'Where is George?' Rocky asked. 'I haven't seen him in a while.'

'Ah, well that's something I could do with advice on.'

'Oh is this still about his job?' Elvis asked.

'No, I actually found out about his job, but it went a bit wrong.' I explained what happened.

'Are you telling me that you, George and the puppy ended up at the hospital?' Rocky sounded incredulous, I realised it did sound more than a little bizarre.

'And you went on a bus?' Nellie narrowed her eyes.

'I've never been on a bus,' Oliver said. 'In all my days.'

'Most cats haven't,' Elvis added. 'Although I did go on a bus once with my owner a long time ago—'

'Guys, I get this is a strange story but the fact is we all got home safely, I know that we got caught and Claire had to be called . . . Anyway, the thing is that George's job is visiting Harold and his friends in hospital and now he's furious with me because he can't go anymore. He said I have made him lose his job.'

'You have messed it up for him a bit,' Nellie pointed out.

'I know, I know, and I feel like the worst father in the world but I was worried about him. And actually, if you'd seen the journey and the risks he took, you wouldn't be happy with him going either.'

'And I guess it wasn't exactly your fault that Pickles followed you,' Rocky said.

'But, now everyone's mad at me and I need to put things right. But I need to put it right with George first.'

'Alfie,' Nellie said, gently. 'He's been through enough lately, not just losing Tiger but also with Harold in hospital.' Her tone was gentle, but she was right.

'I know, I've got an idea. How about you get him his job back,' Oliver said.

'That's a lovely suggestion but how can I do that?' I asked, feeling panicked. If only Tiger were here, I thought suddenly and with a pang, she always knew what to do. Or if she didn't she would at least keep me calm. At the moment I was anything but calm.

'Right, let's think about this logically,' Rocky suggested, putting a paw on me, he was doing his best, they all were and I was grateful for my friends. Remember, how lucky I am, I kept telling myself. I might be in the dog house right now but I was still lucky.

'Have I got this right?' Elvis said. 'George's job was visiting Harold in hospital?' he said proudly.

'Chip off the old block,' I said.

'Yes, Alfie, what would you do if you could do anything to put this right?' Elvis said.

'I would make it so George could visit Harold in hospital again,' I said. 'Like Oliver suggested.'

'So that's what you have to do,' Nellie said.

'But how? The humans will be so cross if he sneaks off again . . . Maybe I could get one of them to take George when they visit Harold.'

'But I thought the hospital said that cats weren't allowed?' Oliver pointed out. He was a clever cat, I could see Nellie blushing a little when he spoke.

'Maybe the hospital would change their mind if they saw how happy the patients are when he's there? Now who would be the best person to take him?' I started thinking carefully, running through all my humans in my head. Not Claire, she was too angry, Jonathan only went straight from work, as did Polly and Matt. Sylvie was unlikely to be convinced either . . . It only left Marcus, and he was a bit of a pushover – perfect.

'OK, so how do I get Marcus to take George?' I asked.

'When you want a human to take you somewhere, you just follow them,' Nellie reminded me.

'Yes but that's what got George into this mess in the first place – unless, Nellie, you're a genius! If I get George to follow Marcus, but make it clear he's following him, Marcus will have no choice but to take George with him. Of course that's it!'

'All in a day's work for us, Alfie,' Rocky said.

'Now all you have to do is to sell the plan to George,' Nellie pointed out.

'That'll be a breeze, well if I get him to listen to me long enough to tell him.'

'Goodness me, you are an interesting bunch of cats,' Oliver said. 'I've barely been here for a minute and already it's more exciting than my old life.' He looked quite thrilled.

'So, Oliver, how did you get to be in a shelter?' I asked.

'I was telling your friends earlier, my old family had a problem and couldn't look after me anymore. I'm not sure exactly what happened but it was very sad.'

'I'm sorry to hear that,' I said, he needed good friends.

'The shelter was very kind to us, and the staff were wonderful, they took good care of us. When the Barkers came in to adopt me, well, I felt like the luckiest cat in the world. I'm not young, or cute like a kitten but I am a nice cat.'

'I can see that,' I said, feeling emotional. 'And I'm so happy that the Barkers have you now as well.'

'Not so keen on you though, Alfie,' Rocky joked.

'No, I got chased out of their house a fair few times when I broke in to see Tiger,' I said. I felt like I had a new friend, and a new plan to get back into my George's good books. Life was looking up.

Now I just had to get George to agree to the plan, and before that I had to get him to get close enough to me so I could tell him the plan. Which wasn't easy.

'Go away,' he hissed later that evening as I approached him.

'George, I really need to talk to you, I need to put this right.'

'Too late, I'm going out,' he said and off he ran. I thought about following him but that was what got me into this mess in the first place. Hana might be able to relay my plan to George if he refused to listen to me? I crossed my paws that I would be able to make this plan work.

Chapter
Twenty-One

I managed to go to Hana's early the following morning without George noticing, he was too busy trying to avoid me. And Claire was too busy shouting at Jonathan about the fact that he had to go on a work trip so she would be left holding the fort for a few days. I wasn't happy about their argument, but it was on the hold list for now, because my first priority was to fix things for George.

I clattered against the cat flap to announce my arrival and then I hopped in. Connie saw me first.

'Alfie, how nice to see you,' she said scooping me up. Thank goodness, someone who was happy to see me. 'I hear you've been in a bit of trouble,' she continued stroking my head. I purred loudly to show her how much I was enjoying it.

'Connie, you need to get ready for school,' I heard Sylvie shout, she didn't sound happy either. Connie sighed, put me down and then left, so I went to see Hana who was looking out of the back patio door.

'Hey, Alfie,' she said, in her sweet way.

'Hana, I'm not sure I'm welcome here,' I started, carefully.

'You're always welcome, Alfie, I know George isn't exactly pleased with you, but I am your friend too.'

'That's an understatement about George.'

'Well, you know what he's like, he'll cool off soon enough.'

'I wish I felt as confident as you sound,' I said. 'But I'm here because I need to put things right—' I heard shouting. 'Is that Sylvie?'

'Oh yes, she's not happy at the moment. I heard her say to Marcus that she is tired, and snappy but she thinks that it's something that all women go through at a certain age. And now she feels sick so she thinks she's got a bug as well.'

'It doesn't sound nice. But is it serious?'

'I don't think so, not like Harold, but it's not fun. I heard her tell Claire that if she carried on like this Marcus would run for the hills.'

Claire, Polly and Franceska were all of a similar age, so I wondered if it would happen to my other human friends too. Was that why Claire was so angry today? Another one for my hold list.

'It seems there is a lot going on at the moment. But I have always said we should deal with one thing at a time, so firstly can I talk to you about George.'

'Of course. He misses his job, Alfie, and he's missing Harold, but I think he'll calm down soon.'

'I was going to suggest that he go back to see Harold but he needs to get Marcus to take him.'

'Oh, I hadn't thought of that. But how can he get Marcus to take him?'

'That's why I want to talk to him, but he won't listen. I thought that if he followed Marcus when he went to see Harold one day, but made it obvious, so that Marcus knew he was following him, and then Marcus won't have any choice but to take him with him.' It sounded so simple when I said it out loud, but I knew that the execution might not be as simple.

'What if Marcus says no?' Hana asked.

'I had thought of that, but Marcus is a softy, if George

looks at him with those big eyes of his, he won't be able to resist. Or so I hope. I mean George has to make a big fuss of following Marcus and possibly make a racket to show him how much he wants to go with him, but . . .'

'It's not a bad idea, Alfie, do you want me to talk to George for you?' Hana offered, in her sweet voice.

'Would you?' I asked, raising my whiskers, hopefully.

'Of course, I don't think George should be cross with you all the time, and I have tried to tell him that. It's understandable for a parent to worry.'

'Thanks, Hana, I appreciate it. I better go home for breakfast, but if there's anything I can do to help with the Sylvie situation, please let me know. Once I've sorted George out anyway.'

'Thanks, Alfie.'

We briefly touched noses and said goodbye. At least I had another ally.

Bizarrely Sylvie was at our house by the time I got home, I stopped on the way to play with some leaves, every cat needs to indulge in hobbies. Claire was back from the school run, Pickles was asleep in his bed, George was nowhere to be seen.

'I'm going to the doctor in a couple of days, I'm pretty sure I'm going through the menopause.'

'Oh Sylvie, it'll be good to know, and of course get something to help you. I don't know how I'd cope, because I'm so stressed at the moment I'd probably explode.'

'Things no better with Jon's work?'

'No, worse actually. You know how many times he's told me it's going to get better? Millions, and I'm bored of shouting at him, it's getting beyond a joke. What with Christmas coming soon, it's just a lot.'

'Oh Claire, what a pair we are at the moment, what with Harold in hospital I feel so guilty for snapping at Marcus but I can't control myself. Do you think we should do something?'

'What?'

'How about we get Franceska and Polly and organise a spa day? You know we probably all could do with a day off. And I can always organise for Connie and Aleksy to help with the kids?'

'Oh my goodness, that sounds like bliss, I could really do with that. Yes, I'll tell Jonathan tonight, and get the others on board.'

'Oh hey, Alfie,' Sylvie said, as I hopped on her lap. She gave my head a nice scratch and I purred.

'I still haven't quite forgiven him for the whole hospital escapade,' Claire said.

'I know, and I still have no idea how they managed it but Marcus said that Harold is miserable and he wants to see George.'

My ears pricked up, this was good news indeed, because it meant that Marcus really wouldn't be able to resist George's pleas, if we played it right. I could only hope that Hana convinced him to speak to me or at least listen to the plan.

'Anyway, I'm off to work now, but I'll let you know how I get on when I finally see the doctor.' Sylvie gently placed me on the floor and stood up.

'Call me.' Claire kissed her goodbye. 'Do you think I should see a doctor?' She sounded serious and I rubbed her legs. I hated it when Claire wasn't happy. I hated it when anyone was unhappy but Claire had been my first friend on Edgar Road – her happiness was entwined with mine in many ways.

'No, but I think when Jonathan gets back from this business trip you two need to have a serious talk about how you are going to make more time for the family. You love each other too much not to sort it out.'

'You're right, thanks, and I'll think it through before I shout as well.'

Progress was being made on all sides, paws crossed.

I had played hide and seek, ball and goodness knows what else with Pickles after Sylvie left, in an effort to wear him out. I ended up worn out though, but thankfully we both had a nap together, curled up on the sofa, because I could barely keep my eyes open. After the stress of the past few days, I could have used the cat equivalent of a spa day.

When I woke up, I stretched, and gently nudged Pickles who was still snoring, loudly I may add. The bigger he got, the noisier he seemed to become. Pickles didn't stir, so I got up and went to the kitchen where I found George eating out of his bowl. My heart filled with love the way it did every time I saw him. I stood and watched for a moment, drinking him in. How I wished we could get back to the way we were.

He turned and looked at me.

'Dad,' he said.

'Oh George,' I replied. He came up and nuzzled me and it felt amazing.

'I know I was angry but it wasn't really your fault. Well it was, but I know that you only did what you did because you love me,' he said, sounding so mature.

'You don't know how happy your words make me. Have you spoken to Hana?'

'Yes, and she told me about your conversation. I would like, more than anything, to go and see Harold, but I also realise how much of a risk I was taking now. I mean if I got caught, I might not have ever seen you again.'

'George, you know that would never happen. Remember when you were catnapped? I didn't stop until I found you.'

'I know and if it hadn't been for Pickles . . .'

'Yeah we might have got away with it, although that mean woman's face when she saw him with the children was quite funny.'

'It was and the whole ward did love him. And you. But you see what I mean, there are lots of lonely people out there and it was nice to do something about that.'

'And I am so proud of you for it, George. But listen, I think we can get Marcus to take you to see Harold. He told Marcus he misses you.'

'He does?'

'Yes, Hana told me that she heard Marcus telling Sylvie that. So all you have to do is to figure out when he's going to the hospital, and basically get under his feet. If you make a lot of noise he'll know you are following him.'

'I think I can do that.' George sounded excited again.

'I know you can, son,' I replied.

The first part of the plan was in action. It was time to figure out part two.

Pickles suddenly appeared. He was snuffling around, waddling along, and wagging his tail at us.

'George, I haven't seen you in ever such a long time, and I miss you,' Pickles said.

'I'm sorry, Pickles, I've been swamped but I'm here now. So you can choose what you want to do, and I mean anything,' George said.

'I want to learn to climb trees again, it's been such a long time since I practised that aspect of catting. I'm big now so I'm pretty sure I can climb trees.'

'OK, come on then, race you to the back garden,' George said, shooting off, with Pickles running as fast as he could behind him. For a fat puppy he was actually quite fast.

As I watched my boy – and my new boy – going, I felt my heart soar. Things were going to be alright, I could feel it in my bones. But I also knew there was no way Pickles would be any better at climbing trees.

Chapter
Twenty-Two

The day arrived when we'd try to get Marcus to take George to hospital with him. I prayed it would work, while George hopped around with nerves. He'd got up very early, washed carefully, before having breakfast and then washing himself again. I led him into the garden, for a last-minute pep talk.

'You know what you're doing?' I asked.

'Can we just go through it one more time?' George asked as we shivered in the garden. The plan I had come up with was incredibly detailed, if I did say so myself.

'Right, we know that Marcus is going to the hospital this morning, Hana confirmed that. So you go and wait outside Hana's house, and the minute he comes through the front door you pounce on him. Make as much noise as you can to ensure he knows you're following him. If he tells you to go home, ignore him, even if you end up at the bus stop with him, stay as close to his feet as you can.' It was foolproof.

'What if he picks me up and brings me home?' George asked. Not quite foolproof then.

'Then follow him again. You have to show him that you mean business and there is no way you are going to give up.' Persistence was key.

'Are you going to come with me?' George asked.

'No, son, this is your job and I will help and support you in any way but I know you need to do this on your own.' I was learning as a parent too, you see.

'Thanks, Dad.'

'And I'll be here when you get back, hopefully with a successful visit under your tail.'

I had to occupy myself while George was out, keeping myself busy, because I needed to prove to George that I was able to trust him. Of course I had Pickles for company. Since the back gate had been secured and Claire had more or less forgiven me, she was happier to leave Pickles in my charge once again. As Pickles grew up, he settled down a bit too. He still had a crazy side. He licked everything, even things no cat would ever dream of licking, and he still believed he could be a cat.

His training wasn't going that well though. Even Summer's shouting didn't faze him anymore. He would stand when told to sit, and sit when told to come.

'Pickles,' I said, when he came to find me. George had been gone a good while without coming home so I was pretty sure the plan had worked. I hoped it had, because it would make George happy and also make things so much better between us.

'Alfie, look what I can do,' Pickles replied. He put his front paws up on the sofa and wiggled his bottom and his tail. He had his very cute face on, with hopeful eyes.

'That's great, Pickles, what's it for?' I asked.

'I do it when the kids are eating and they feed me,' he replied. No wonder he was growing so much.

'Remember when we went to the hospital?' I said.

'I will never forget it,' he replied.

'Wasn't the best part when we made everyone happy,' I continued, a warm feeling spreading into my heart.

'Yes, it was. Although the other best part was the bus. I liked the bus,' he said.

'I wasn't so keen on the bus, but seeing the patients looking happy was amazing.'

'It was worth the trouble we got into then?' Pickles asked.

'Yes it was, I guess especially as we didn't get hurt. Apart from when the bus passenger trod on my tail.'

'I don't mind being in trouble, it happens a lot. The other day Polly gave me a bath.' Pickles licked the sofa, and I shuddered. Baths were perhaps my least favourite thing. Or anything to do with water to be fair.

'And?' I asked.

'Oh yes, I jumped out and got her soaking wet and she told me off. But then she laughed and hugged me. It seems being in trouble can be a good thing sometimes.'

'You're learning,' I replied, proud of how well he was turning out.

It didn't last. As I was fretting, I took my eyes off Pickles. I don't know how long it was before I realised that he was gone, but I searched the house and because I wasn't thinking too clearly I didn't even think about the garden. I jumped through the cat flap, and lo and behold there was Pickles, his brown fur covered in mud. The rain was coming down now as well, so it was sticking to him. The worst thing was that he was busily digging up Claire's favourite rose bush, and I knew she wouldn't be happy. I had no choice but to brave the rain, and joined him.

'Stop, Pickles, Claire will be so cross,' I said.

'Why?' he asked. We still hadn't quite got out of the 'why' phase.

'Because that's Claire's favourite rose bush and you're making a mess of it. And you look a wreck.' I shivered, it was cold, wet and miserable. And now I was beginning to resemble a drowned rat. That would teach me to not pay attention. 'Come on, let's try to put the earth back,' I commanded. As we did, I realised that putting it back wasn't as easy as digging it up, despite our best efforts. Well, mine, because Pickles was too busy seeing how much more mud and earth he could get stuck to his fur.

'Why were you digging anyway?' I asked, exasperated by my lack of progress.

'I wanted to go out, like we did the other day but the gate was closed so I thought if I dug up here I could get under the fence.'

'Pickles, you would have to dig for hours to get anywhere close. All you've done is made a mess of the garden, and of yourself.' I was beyond exasperated.

'Oh have I?' He was so innocent, I couldn't stay angry with him, a little like I used to be with George. Babies were just too cute sometimes.

'Yes, you have.' But I grinned. 'Maybe we should give up and go inside, this rain is horrible.'

'Is it?' Again he looked at me with his innocent eyes and I ushered him inside.

We sat on the back doormat, trying to shake the water off us. Before long Claire appeared, and did a double take.

'What on earth have you two been up to? Stay there, don't move a paw and I'll be back.'

Pickles glanced over at me, and I nodded. We should definitely do as we're told when Claire has that tone of voice on her. She returned with some towels and began drying us off in turn. I had managed to stay relatively clean, but was wet, whereas Pickles had black patches of earth all over his fur.

'Right, Alfie, you find somewhere warm to dry off, but this one is coming to have a bath.' She rubbed me in the towel a bit more, before she wrapped Pickles up in the other one and carried him off.

Yet again I was in trouble for something that I was trying to put right. Goodness knows what she'd say when she saw the rose bush.

I made sure I was properly dry before I went into the living room. Claire brought Pickles down, all clean and put him in his bed.

'Stay in that bed,' she commanded. 'I'm going to get the kids but due to this awful rain I'm going to drive.' She set off.

'Are you alright?' I asked, as Pickles sat up in his bed and panted, excitedly.

'I might dig in the garden again another day,' he said.

'Pickles, why would you do that, you just got into trouble?'

'It doesn't feel like trouble, because I had a bath and I really like baths.'

I had no words.

Thankfully, he settled down for another nap, although I didn't dare take my eyes off him in case he headed out into the garden again. Just as I felt that my eyes would explode, or more likely close by themselves, the front door opened and in bounded the children.

Henry and Martha ran up to Pickles and rudely woke him

up by grabbing him. Toby and Summer hovered behind, wanting their turn. Then I was delighted to see Marcus carrying George in his arms. He put him on the floor, and Marcus followed Claire into the kitchen.

'Everything alright,' I asked George.

'Never better, Dad, come into the kitchen, I want to hear what Marcus says.' We both ran in.

'I can't believe you took George to the hospital,' Claire said, she sounded more surprised than angry though.

'He didn't give me much choice. He followed me out this morning, and he also kept standing on my feet. I tried to get him to come home but he just yowled at me and then stuck to me like glue. I was going to phone you but I was running late, so I just took him with me.'

'What did they say at the hospital?'

'Luckily it was Jay in charge of the ward today, so I explained how much Dad was missing him and he said it was on me, and he'd turn a blind eye if I promised he'd behave. Dad was over the moon, he had tears in his eyes. Then he got me to do the rounds with George, so he could visit other patients. Claire, you wouldn't believe how happy George made everyone. Dad gave me a lecture on how lonely some of the patients are and how much of a difference a cuddle from George can make.'

'That's amazing, and I guess my cats have always known how to cheer people up.' Claire sounded quite emotional. 'Alfie always did when he first came here to me as a kitten. I've been worrying about how much Harold has told us about the lonely people for a while actually. Can I help in any way?'

'Ah, I'm so glad you asked.' Marcus smiled. Marcus was tall, and he had glasses and sometimes he could look serious, but he had the kindest smile. 'I was going to ask if you'd be my partner in crime and take George into the hospital with you when you visit Dad. I know it's asking a lot, because you're breaking goodness knows how many rules but . . .'

'Of course I will. We can draw up a roster if you like, but I draw the line at taking Alfie and Pickles too.'

'Meow,' I objected, hopping onto Claire's lap. 'But then seeing the state the pair of them were in this afternoon, it might be safer.'

'What did they do?'

Just then the doorbell rang, and we all followed Claire to answer it. Pickles was there first, wiggling his bottom excitedly. Sylvie stood on the doorstep. She didn't look good. Her hair was soaking wet and sticking to her head, and she looked as if she'd been crying.

'Oh you're wet through, come in,' Claire said.

'No, no, I won't,' Sylvie snapped. Pickles lost interest and went back to the living room to play with the children. Sylvie looked angry now and Claire alarmed. I went to get Marcus.

'What is it, Alfie?' he said.

'Yowl,' I replied, come with me. Just then Claire called him, and he finally got the message. We walked to the front door, and he stopped short when he saw Sylvie.

'What on earth?'

'I should have known you'd be here,' Sylvie snapped.

'Well funny story, George—'

'There's nothing funny about this, actually,' Sylvie said. 'I knew you two are always together these days but do you think I'm stupid?' she snapped.

I had seen this side of Sylvie before, the one who was so upset about her divorce that she was angry with everyone. It wasn't my favourite Sylvie and I had no idea what was going on.

'Sylvie, what are you talking about?' Claire asked.

'My best friend, not to mention next door neighbour having an affair with my boyfriend,' she spat.

'What's an affair?' Summer asked, having appeared suddenly. Claire's eyes widened in horror as did mine and Marcus's. George looked confused. 'And what's for tea, I'm hungry?' Summer added.

Even Sylvie looked a little shamefaced as Marcus shrugged at Claire and then went outside, gently taking Sylvie by the arm and shutting our door behind them. Just what on earth was going on?

'Finally, we're on our own,' I said to George. It had been a long evening. Claire was so upset about what Sylvie said, which still made no sense.

But that would have to wait, because I wanted to hear from George himself about his hospital visit.

'I loved going to see Harold,' George said. 'He was so pleased to see me, and so was everyone else, it is so good to be doing my job again.'

'And by the sound of it, you'll be doing it without any risk now as Claire and Marcus are both going to take you to see Harold. So it's a great outcome.'

'Yes, but he's not going to be in hospital much longer. He's coming out soon, they said.'

'Really? Marcus didn't mention that, but then he got interrupted by Sylvie.'

'Yes, she seemed a bit crazy,' he said.

'We shouldn't say crazy, George,' I chastised. 'But she was upset about something and although we know that Marcus and Claire are just friends, something must have triggered it.'

'Well Harold is coming home, I think in a couple of weeks. And then it's going to be nearly Christmas,' he said. 'Then I'll be unemployed.'

'It is.' We weren't in December yet, but November was underway. 'Although, George, you will have a job visiting Harold at home and making sure he's OK.'

'I know, but after Harold comes out of hospital, I think we should find a way to help lonely people still,' George said.

'You are the most wonderful kitten a cat could ever ask for,' I said, meaning it.

'I'm not a kitten anymore,' George said, leaning over and swiping me with his paw.

'You'll always be my kitten,' I finished.

I settled George into bed, and then went to Claire's room where she and Jonathan were getting ready for bed.

'It's crazy, but Marcus phoned me after and said that Sylvie had calmed down, and that he or she would explain everything tomorrow.'

'What brought that on? I mean I don't have to worry about you and Marcus do I?' Jonathan laughed, showing that he was joking.

'Darling, of course you don't, I'm too busy looking after your children, your pets and other people to do anything, and you know how much I love you anyway.'

'And you're a saint to put up with me,' Jonathan said, giving her a hug. 'But the good news is that my deputy is fully in place, and he's so ambitious that he's snapping at my heels, if he wants to try to get my job he might actually do a lot of my work.' He laughed.

'So not worried about him actually taking your job then?' Claire raised an eyebrow. 'Only you could see him as an asset rather than a rival!'

'No, it's fine, we're both on the same page, he has a bit to learn but he's keen and hard-working. I've said that I will be home for bath and bedtime for the kids every night unless it's pre-arranged and I think now things are settling down we should make sure we have our date nights as well. I know I haven't been the best husband and father the last few months but I will put that right now.'

'Oh Jon, I do love you.'

I left with a grin on my face, and took myself to bed. I curled up, and thought about the day. So much had happened, it had been ridiculously busy, a mixture of good and bad. And as I prepared to drift into sleep I hoped that it would be a calmer day tomorrow.

Chapter
Twenty-Three

It was lunchtime before the mystery of Sylvie's outburst was finally solved. George, Pickles and I were tucking into our food when we heard.

Claire had been to the supermarket in the morning, and then she popped in to see Harold, but without George as she went straight from the supermarket. George, Pickles and I had spent a lazy morning at home, and even Pickles failed to get into trouble. George, still on a high from having been to hospital the previous day, was happy to entertain Pickles and I was happy to sit back and relax for once. We heard the letter box flap on the door and Pickles scooted as fast as he could to the door. He barked his little bark, constantly, and sat with his back to the door as a shower of letters landed on his head. It was one of his favourite pastimes. George laughed, as did I. Shortly after, the door opened, Claire walked in with Sylvie, who looked nice and normal again. Claire picked up the post, Sylvie picked up Pickles and we made our way to the kitchen.

'Are you sure you don't mind me coming in?' Sylvie asked. Her hair was neat, pulled back off her face and she had make-up on.

'Come in, apart from anything else I want to know what on earth was going on yesterday?' Claire said. She didn't sound cold, but she didn't sound as warm as normal either as she put our food down and we all tucked in.

'You know I went to the doctor the other day?' Sylvie

asked. Claire nodded. 'They did some tests and yesterday I got the results. It freaked me out a bit.'

'Oh no, nothing serious, I hope?' Claire gestured for Sylvie to sit down. 'Coffee?'

'No, I better not. And as for serious, it depends on your point of view. Claire, I'm pregnant.'

Now, I definitely hadn't seen that coming. I didn't know how old Sylvie was exactly but she seemed about the same age as Claire.

A massive smile appeared on Claire's face. 'Oh my goodness, Sylvie, you're pregnant! I can't believe it.'

'Neither can I! I'm in my forties and Connie's fifteen for goodness' sake. And when I found out yesterday I freaked out. I had all these thoughts running wild in my head. What if Marcus was angry with me? I mean we never thought children were on the cards, never discussed it. I thought that I was going through the menopause for goodness' sake. And then I worried about what Connie would think, her father has just had another baby, so what if it felt as if we were both replacing her. I felt totally out of control, terrified and confused and then when I couldn't get hold of Marcus and then found out he was at your house, I just lost it.'

'You certainly did, but, Sylvie, it's a big deal, I just wish you'd said something.'

'I told Marcus on your doorstep and he was so happy that any fears I had immediately melted away and then I felt like a total fool. And then he persuaded me to tell Connie straight away and she hugged me and said that she was so happy because it meant she would worry about me less, if that made sense, and also that she would be a great big sister. I cried so much, I didn't have any tears left. And tonight we're going to the hospital, Marcus and I, to tell Harold. You must think I'm such a fool.' Sylvie wiped tears from her cheeks.

'No, I think you're amazing, and lucky. Imagine when I first met you you felt as if you'd lost everything but Connie and Hana, and you were pretty miserable. But then we all got our friendship back and you met Marcus and you have barely stopped smiling since. I think it's amazing and you know we will all help out.'

'That explains why I was so up and down lately, it was hormones, just not in the way I thought it was! But you know I am excited. I'm scared, there could be all sorts of issues, but Marcus and I talked well into the night and the thing is I know he's committed to me and to Connie and the baby. In fact he made me book a scan first thing, because he said that the sooner I have a scan the sooner my mind might be at rest, he really is thoughtful.'

'I can't believe it, my head is spinning,' Claire laughed and then she grabbed Sylvie and hugged her.

'I am so happy, Claire. I mean I know I accused you of having an affair with Marcus yesterday and I am so sorry but, as I said, I wasn't quite in my right mind.'

'Will Marcus finally move into your house now?' Claire asked.

'Yes, we talked about that. I need him but then that leaves Harold on his own, so we need to figure that out. Harold values his independence as you know so I don't think he'd move in with us but we have to sort something out.'

'Of course, there'll be so many plans to make,' Claire said, beaming.

'I would crack open the champagne but you know, I can't drink . . .'

'I'll have a glass tonight for both of us.' The two women hugged again.

I told George to go and see Hana, after all she needed to be congratulated too, she was going to have a new human soon.

Claire took Pickles out for a walk, while George went next door, and I decided to have forty, well-deserved winks.

When George came back, he asked if I would take a walk with him.

'Sure, where do you want to go?' I asked.

'To see our other friends, since my job I've hardly had any time with them.' I knew how he felt, since I had been put in charge of Pickles I had seen less of my friends than usual. Both the Edgar Road cats and dear Dustbin. However, we had a meal at Franceska and Tomasz's restaurant on Sunday, for family day so I would see plenty of Dustbin then.

'They'll be so pleased to see you,' I agreed.

'Oh my goodness, it's so long since we've seen you together,' Nellie said, gleefully greeting us with a nuzzle.

'And it's great that you're all here,' I said as I greeted Elvis and Rocky.

'The gang is back together,' Elvis said. 'Right, can you please fill us in on all the news,' he added.

We told them the latest hospital news, and of course about the baby, and then Rocky and George went off to climb George's favourite tree.

'You're forgiven now then?' Nellie asked.

'Thankfully, yes, I hated it when he wasn't talking to me,

but it's been so hectic lately I haven't had much time to really process anything.'

'Are you alright though, Alfie?' Elvis asked.

'I'm getting there,' I replied, honestly. Oliver joined us. 'Hi,' I said, greeting him warmly.

'I really love it here, although I'll love it more in the summer,' Oliver said.

'I hear you,' Nellie said.

'George,' I shouted as I saw him and Rocky near the bottom of the tree. 'Come here.'

'Oh, we haven't met have we?' George said as he approached.

'No, but I've heard all about you,' Oliver said. 'And I am very delighted to meet you.'

'And I'm happy to meet you. How are you settling in?' George asked, he was so sweet, my heart was bursting with pride for my boy.

'Pretty well. I know you know my house very well, and I hope you don't find it too hard me being there,' Oliver asked.

'No, because Tiger mum taught me how to be kind and being kind means that you want everyone to be happy. The Barkers were very lonely without a cat.'

'Yes, they said that to me when they got me, that a home isn't a home without a cat. And I am grateful for a loving home, it doesn't happen for every cat.'

'So, basically the Barkers aren't lonely anymore and neither are you,' George said.

'Exactly right,' Oliver replied.

'But you know we are all so lucky to have each other,'

I said, suddenly. 'We are all good friends and with Oliver, a new friend, and we'll never be lonely with each other either.'

'Friendship makes the world go round,' Rocky said.

'I thought that was love.' Nellie looked confused.

'They are pretty much the same thing I think,' Elvis finished. And I looked at my friends, old and new, and I knew it was time to count my blessings again. I was so lucky I didn't need to worry about loneliness and it was a real shame that anyone in the whole wide world had to feel it.

'Dad, I've got the answer,' George said suddenly.

'To what?' I asked.

'Harold, when he comes home from hospital and Marcus moves in with Sylvie, I worry that he might be lonely.'

'But, George, he's got all of us and our families, we'll see him all the time.'

'Yes, but when he goes to sleep, he won't have anyone else in the house with him. And when he wakes up. He'll be all alone then. And I can't move in with him because Toby needs me . . .'

'Yes, George, but from what I've heard he wants to live in his own house.'

'So we need to make sure he's not alone,' George stated, pulling himself up to his full height and looking quite pleased with himself. 'Harold needs a cat of his own.'

As we walked home, we discussed the idea some more.

'But, George, won't you be jealous, after all you and Harold have a special bond and you would have to share him.'

'I've learnt to share an awful lot lately; with Pickles and now seeing Oliver in Tiger mum's house . . . I really don't want to be selfish about it, and it makes perfect sense. Harold needs a cat. I would suggest giving him Pickles but then I thought that Henry and Martha might not like it, so we need to get him a cat of his own.'

'OK, it's not a bad idea, but how on earth do we put it into practice? It's not as if we just happen to have a spare cat laying around.' I grinned.

'I know, on Sunday the adults said they are going to discuss what the options are for Harold, we will have to listen and then you'll have to show them that the answer is a cat. It's simple really.'

For him maybe, just how the hell was I going to do that? I needed yet another plan. Honestly my skills were being put to the test lately.

Chapter
Twenty-Four

Chapter
Twenty-Four

Family day is one of my favourite days ever because I get nearly everyone I love under one roof. And when it's at Franceska and Tomasz's restaurant, I get to see Dustbin which is a big bonus. I could do with some of his wisdom, now I had been charged somehow with getting Harold a cat. And George, my lovely George, assumed that I would be able to do it. Sometimes children seemed to think parents could do anything, and although that was flattering, it was also a lot of pressure.

However, I couldn't let him down, not after everything we had been through lately. But I had no idea how I was going to do it yet. Harold was finally due out of hospital the following week. Talk had turned to the fact that Sylvie, now pregnant, needed Marcus around more than ever, but Harold wouldn't entertain moving in with them – he wanted to be in his own home. The doctors said he would be able to live alone, as long as he had help, which of course he did but George had already said he didn't want him to be alone late at night or in the morning, when we wouldn't be there for him.

'George, I get that you don't want Harold to be lonely and I will do all I can to put your plan into action,' I said. 'But I can't make any promises.'

'I know you'll do it,' George said, leaving me no choice.

We set off and more excitedly, because Hana was joining us, although Connie was carrying her, and Pickles was also with us, although he was on a lead so there was no way he could get into trouble. Even so, he kept splashing into puddles, left by last night's rain, which made Polly a little annoyed, Matt seemed to find it funny. Until he got soaked of course.

We all arrived at the restaurant, and everyone greeted each other with hugs and kisses, as coats were taken off, scarfs and gloves discarded. The children ran to Tommy, begging him to play a game with them and Pickles and George. Tommy said he would set up a little course for them. Aleksy and Connie immediately sneaked off together, so George, Hana and I headed to the back of the restaurant to find Dustbin.

'I don't know if I want to go outside, it's cold,' Hana said.

'Just for a bit and I promise if you want to come back in, I'll come with you,' George coaxed.

'OK, I do want to see Dustbin after all.'

We made our way out and found Dustbin cleaning his paws in the yard.

'Ah hello, friends.' He came and greeted us. 'It's been far too long.'

'I know, there has been so much going on, we'll fill you in, where's Ally?' I asked.

'Oh she'll be along later, she just went for a walk. I was waiting for you guys, but sometimes Ally gets a bit stir crazy in the yard and needs to get out – not sure why it's a mighty fine yard.' We all looked around the yard, it was spacious but a bit gloomy and there were a lot of big bins out here. I could see why you might want to spend a bit of time away from it.

'I'm going to get Harold a cat,' George announced and then we filled Dustbin in on our plans.

'I think it's a grand idea,' Dustbin said when he finished. 'But short of kidnapping a cat for him, I'm not sure how to do it.'

'And we don't have the first idea how to kidnap a cat, not that we would ever do that of course,' I pointed out.

'Yes, that wouldn't be right, I mean I want Harold to have the company as well, I think it's a very good idea, but not if we have to steal a cat,' Hana added.

We all gave it some thought.

'I know, I've got it,' I said and I really did. 'What if there was away to lead a homeless cat to Harold's.' It was a brilliant idea, if I did say so myself.

'But how will we find this homeless cat?' Hana asked.

'Dustbin can ask about, and Ally too. You never know there might be a cat around who would be glad of a warm home.' It did make sense. To me anyway.

'We can certainly ask around,' Dustbin said, 'but I don't know . . . I mean most of the outside cats we know like it that way. Anyway, if we do hear of anyone I'll let you know.' He sounded uncertain and my confidence took a slight knock. Ally arrived and I relayed my plan to her.

'I'm not sure how easy it will be, but we can try,' she said, sounding a little more upbeat than Dustbin. I would take that. 'But, Alfie, you might need to have another idea as well,' she suggested gently. OK, so as usual I needed a backup plan.

Hana went inside shortly afterwards, as it was too cold for her, and George went with her. I guessed they would join in with the children. I took a few moments to have a deeper chat with Dustbin and Ally about George's fixation with loneliness.

'I understand it, I do. I remember feeling lonely even when I wasn't alone, after Snowball . . .' Snowball was my first love, when she and her family moved away it was devastating. 'Then after Tiger, but I did have family and friends around me, so I have to acknowledge that. Harold does too, although he does live alone and I can see why that would worry George.'

'I think, Alfie, George really saw his hospital visits as his job, and now he knows that is coming to an end, he's turning his efforts elsewhere. First Harold and then, well, like you he'll want to make sure no one is ever lonely again.'

'So all this is my fault really?'

'I'm afraid so. You brought up a fine young tom, and now he wants to do good in the world. We can't complain about that can we?'

'And you know he has a point. I heard people talking about how hard it is to be on their own, and look at your families in the restaurant, they're all happy. It would be wonderful if there was more of that in the world,' Ally said. 'Even Dustbin and I found each other, before that I was a loner.'

'You're right, and although we might not be able to fix the loneliness problems of the world we can try to do our bit, right?'

'Right, Alfie.'

I had to do my bit. In our world of Edgar Road, the immediate issue was Harold. What if he got ill in the night? I just hoped if we did get him a cat, it would be almost as smart as us. One of the reasons a dog would be absolutely no good.

Everyone was sat around the table and the hum of easy

chatter filled the restaurant. The children had their own table, although Aleksy and Connie complained that they were grown-up enough to be able to sit with the adults. They weren't quite though, and as Claire pointed out, they were needed to keep the younger ones in check.

'It's good news that your dad is coming home this week,' Franceska said.

'I know, and you guys have been amazing,' Marcus replied. 'Claire and I are drawing up a roster to make sure he's taken care of at home the way he was in hospital. I don't know how I'll ever thank you all.'

'Pah, that's what friends are for. Whenever we can help we can,' Tomasz said, although he was very busy so I wasn't sure how much time he would have.

'We're worried about him being alone though,' Sylvie said. 'I need Marcus with me, especially as the pregnancy isn't that easy.'

'I cannot believe we have another baby coming,' Polly said, she ignored the idea of the difficult pregnancy.

'But my moods are all over the place,' Sylvie said. 'And I'm worried I might, you know, not cope as well as I should,' she added carefully.

'Sylvie, I had postnatal depression with Henry,' Polly said.

'I didn't know that,' Sylvie said. I did, it was when I first met Polly, Matt and Henry, before Martha was in the picture. In fact I may have even diagnosed her postnatal depression myself.

'Yes, it was tough but once I knew what it was, I got help and was fine, so with us around you, you won't fall into any holes. We won't let you.'

'Thanks, guys, but still Harold is resolute he won't move in with us, so we still have the problem of what to do about him.'

'He'll probably be fine,' Jonathan said, uncertainly.

'Yeah,' Matt added. 'The doctors said he's OK to go home and they know he lives alone.'

'I know but it doesn't stop us worrying,' Marcus replied. I glanced over at George, he glanced over at Hana, and I called them in close.

'It's a long shot but I've got an idea. If we all jump up on the table, they might get that we're trying to tell them something,' I suggested. A genius idea if I did say so myself.

'But they hate us being on the table, we always get in trouble,' Hana said.

'Exactly.' George grinned. 'Dad's right, if we do that they will know we're telling them something.'

'Right, let's do it,' I said. The three of us jumped onto laps and then onto the table.

'What on earth are you doing? Get down this minute,' Claire said. I saw Polly try not to laugh at her tone. Polly often said Claire missed her vocation and should have been a school teacher.

'Yowl,' I shouted.

'Yowl,' Hana added.

'Yowl,' George finished.

The adults glanced between us.

'Anyone would think they were trying to tell us something,' Jonathan said. I raised my whiskers, of course we were; humans could be a little slow on the uptake but you would think that after all the years of my teaching, they might have got it by now.

'Maybe they are saying that we should get Harold a cat?' Tomasz suggested.

'Meow,' I said and nuzzled Tomasz to reward him. He was the cleverest right now.

'Meow,' George reiterated.

'Meow,' Hana thirded. The adults all studied us hard. But I think we had managed to convey the message.

'That's it, if Harold had a cat, he wouldn't be quite on his own, and if the cat is anything like these three, they'll take good care of him,' Matt said.

'What a great idea and Dad will love it. As long as George isn't jealous, I mean those two are like best friends.'

'Meow,' George said, to show he didn't mind at all. He then went to Marcus and jumped into his arms to reiterate the point.

'These cats are so clever,' Jonathan said. 'But it is a great idea, if Harold has a cat then at least we know he's got company when we're not there.'

'It's a genius idea,' Claire said.

'After all, everyone needs a cat,' Franceska finished rubbing my ears.

'Woof.' We all turned to see poor Pickles trying to climb up a chair leg but he couldn't. I'd almost forgotten about him in my delight that my plan was working, so I hopped down and went to join him.

'Am I ever going to be a cat, Alfie?' he asked.

'We'll see,' I replied. Which is what adults said when they really meant no.

As the adults discussed the cat they were going to get for Harold, I went to eat. Claire was going to take charge but she liked that, and they said they would of course get an older cat, because the last thing Harold or any of us needed was a kitten. And they had to remember Harold's age but then of course any cat that came to live with him would be part of our family so they would never be alone anyway. I went to tell Dustbin the good news, and I was feeling so proud of us all as I did so. We'd proved to be a formidable team yet again.

Chapter Twenty-Five

It was a year to the day since we lost Tiger, I knew this because Oliver told us the Barkers had been preparing for it. In fact they were going to wait to get Oliver until the year anniversary, as it seemed right, but in the end they had gone to find him a bit earlier.

Because he told us about this day, we decided to make it Tiger day. We'd had a memorial, after Tiger passed away, which I knew nothing about but we learnt to say goodbye to her, and now we were going to honour the year without her by telling her how much we missed her and loved her still. All our friends were meeting at the recreation ground.

George even asked Hana if she would come and she'd agreed. She might not like the cold, or even the outside that much but she was a good cat and a good friend to George. The only problem we had was Pickles.

'Why can't I come?' he had whined as we prepared to leave.

'You know why,' George retorted. 'You can't be out without a human. We've had enough trouble already, what with nearly being run over, and caught at the hospital, don't you think?'

'It's not fair. No matter how hard I work at being a cat I am still a dog.'

'Life isn't fair, my lad,' I said kindly, shooting George a warning look. 'But we will tell you all about it as soon as we get home.'

He turned his back on us in a sulk. Poor Pickles, it was

hard for him but after all he was still only a puppy. We loved him, but there was nothing any of us could do about the 'dogness' of him.

We called for Hana and set off to the meeting place. I was heartened to see that everyone was there already. Dustbin and Ally had even come from the yard, which was touching. Elvis, Nellie and Rocky, my three closest Edgar Road friends, were there, even Salmon had turned up with Oliver – what a wonderful group it was.

'Right,' Elvis said, taking control. 'Let's share our favourite Tiger story, or memory, in order to honour her today,' he said, seriously.

'I'll go first,' I said. 'Everyone knows how much I loved Tiger and how close we were. When we first met though she really didn't like exercise, and I used to make her come for long walks with me, she would complain all the way but then she ended up liking exercise even more than I did.' It was a simple memory but I had others which instead of sharing I wanted to keep in my heart.

'She was my Tiger mum,' George said. 'And I am just proud to have had her in my life and I hope that she's proud of me now.'

'Oh George, she would be beyond proud of you,' I said, through my emotions. 'Everyone is beyond proud of you.'

'Oh good.' He raised his tail, and I felt that he had come such a long way lately.

We all stood solemnly as Rocky recounted how Tiger was a great bird chaser in her time, Nellie talked about the 'girl' chats they shared and how now she was surrounded by boys she missed that the most, Elvis said she could be really feisty when pushed, which she could be, and Salmon said how she never quite liked him and called him a 'busybody' – which to be fair he was. Oliver stayed quiet as did Ally, but Dustbin finished the chat.

'I knew Tiger more through Alfie and then George than first-hand, although I did have the pleasure of meeting her a few times. But what struck me is that she embodied what being a cat was. Yes she was feisty but only really when she was protecting those she loved, she was loyal, she was fun, she was loving and kind, and she had a big heart. Tiger was an example to all of us and by following that example she will always live on through all of us.'

It was a sombre moment as we let those words sink in. Dustbin might be feral but he was incredibly wise. I felt choked, and I nuzzled Dustbin in gratitude for such a wonderful summing up of Tiger . . .

'Woof woof, woof woof,' a voice interrupted us bounding into our group. All the cats sprang back apart from Dustbin, George, Hana and I. They made quite a racket.

'Shush, it's alright,' I told them. 'It's only Pickles.'

'How on earth did you get out?' George asked as Pickles wagged his tail at us.

'I am more cat than you thought,' he replied.

Nellie, Rocky, Oliver and Elvis started moving closer, examining him curiously.

'Claire was in the front garden, talking to someone and so I escaped and then I ran really fast.' Pickles sounded so proud, and George gave him a paw. 'And I knew you came here, because I've been walked past it when you were here before, so I am actually a very clever cat too.'

'High five! Good one, Pickles,' George said, although I really didn't think he should encourage him.

'How many times have we told you not to go out on your own?' I despaired.

'But it's too much fun,' he argued.

'Oh my goodness, what is going on? Bad puppy.' Claire ran up, breathless. She clutched her stomach as if she'd been winded. We all tried to look busy. Nellie started playing with some leaves, Rocky moved to the nearest tree, Dustbin and Ally took a step back and Oliver along with Salmon hid in a bush. 'Do you always meet here?' Claire asked. Although we met here regularly, we were away from the road so the humans didn't know about our patch.

'Meow,' I said. It didn't hurt her to know, after all we weren't doing anything wrong.

'Right, you come with me.' She picked up a wriggling Pickles and walked off. 'See you at home,' she said to George and me. At least this time she couldn't blame me for Pickles' behaviour. I was as bemused as she was, after our back gate had been turned into a fortress. George and I could squeeze under it but poor chubby Pickles . . .

We dispersed soon after, bizarrely a human turning up seemed to unsettle my friends more than the fact that Pickles had. They didn't like outsiders knowing about our special place. I reassured them that Claire would be too angry with Pickles to give it too much thought and we all said our goodbyes.

'We ought to go home, George,' I said. 'Pickles might need us.'

'Yeah, he's in big trouble. Right, Hana, we'll drop you off, and thank you for coming.'

'You know I'd do anything for you,' Hana replied and we all blinked at each other.

Pickles had been told off and was sulking in his bed. Even George couldn't cheer him up, he really was in the doghouse, excuse the pun. After all the emotion of the day, I decided to take a cat nap and enjoy the peace and quiet. I felt sorry for Pickles being in trouble, although I was secretly impressed with his earlier jail break. He really was more cat than I gave him credit for. At least when he was sulking he couldn't get into more trouble, so I was able to sneak away and fall asleep on the sofa.

I was woken by voices, I pricked my ears up and began to open my eyes.

'Are you sure about this?' I heard Jonathan ask. He was home from work extra early and had been making an effort lately, work had eased off as he promised, and it was so nice to have extra time with him. Not least because he brought George and me nice treats to eat. Our house was finally a happy home again.

'Look, Jon, it is weird but it's also fate,' Claire replied.

'I don't believe in fate,' Jonathan replied.

'In this case you should believe in fate. I mean the timing and everything. To think I was making all those phone calls to cat shelters when the answer was right here!'

It was quite cryptic and I had no idea what they were talking about, as I fully opened my eyes and stretched.

'What about Alfie?' Jonathan asked. They both looked at

me and I eyeballed them back. What about me? 'And it's very sad, as well, of course.'

'Alfie'll be happy,' Claire hissed and then directed Jonathan away. 'We can't talk about this in front of him.'

What on earth? Why couldn't they talk about it in front of me, that was what they usually said when they were trying to keep things from the children. I wasn't a child though, I was an adult. I stalked off and joined Pickles in his sulk, while we waited for Matt or Polly to come to collect him. I'd had enough drama for one day.

George and I went out that dark evening, despite the cold and the wind. We looked up at the stars, as the breeze ruffled our fur.

'Do you think Tiger heard us today?' George asked.

'Yes, and I think she would be pleased that we're friends with Oliver,' I added.

'Life is funny isn't it?' George said.

'Yes, it is, when we lose loved ones, we have to let love guide us,' I said, feeling sentimental.

'And with everything that we've been through, with Tiger, with Harold and my hospital job, and Hana being my very best friend, I know that everyone can suffer from loneliness, and that it's the worst thing, and the fact that I've never been lonely means I am the luckiest cat ever. Although I miss Tiger mum, I don't have to be alone ever and even when I'm sad I'm not alone.'

'And the same goes for me. I have been lonely at times, George, but never since I met you of course.'

'So if Harold gets a cat, then we'll be their friend too,' George said.

'Of course, that's what we do, we make friends with everyone, even a dog.' I grinned.

'Pickles isn't so bad. Not for a puppy anyway. Although, thank goodness Harold's getting a cat and not a dog. But, Dad, we'll never have to be lonely will we?'

'No, George, never, and we will always be the lucky ones for that.' I crossed my paws and said a prayer that this would be true.

Chapter Twenty-Six

There was definitely a strange atmosphere in our house. Frustratingly I had no idea what was causing it. And neither did George. We were both being kept in the dark. There had been lots of whispered conversations following the last one I'd heard, and plotting it seemed. I worked out that the humans were making a huge deal out of getting Harold his cat and for some reason it had to be a secret.

'Why can't they just go and get one?' George asked. Harold had been home for a while now and Christmas was approaching, so George really didn't want him to be on his own longer than necessary. Although he was barely left alone and Marcus had got him something called a panic alarm for emergencies. It all sounded very complicated to me, George and I agreed that a cat would be much simpler as a panic button. I just hoped they were trying to get the right cat.

'Perhaps they are making sure that the cat is clever enough,' I pointed out.

'But most cats are clever,' George retorted.

'True, maybe they're making sure it has the right personality for our family. Remember some cats can be a bit moody, and others are a little aggressive, not our friends but outside of our group.'

'All all the cats we know are lovely.'

'Another reason we're lucky,' I pointed out. 'But of course the cat would have to like Pickles as well, and children, as well as old people.'

'You're right, it might be harder than we thought to find a cat like that, just because we are, doesn't mean all cats are. It's quite a list: clever, sociable, lovely, kind, good at plans, likes dogs . . . There probably aren't many cats like that out there.'

'That's true, George.' I felt my fur freeze as the penny dropped. I glanced at George and quickly away. All the secret conversations and the 'don't talk about it in front of Alfie,' ran through my brain. I knew what was going on and I didn't like it, not one little bit. They were going to give me to Harold. They couldn't find another cat like me so they were giving me away. I felt a sense of horror, and dread all mixed up together.

My eyes flickered to George again. How could they even consider separating us? I know it was just the end of the street but this was the home I shared with my son and my main family. I was a doorstep cat, but not one to be given away willy nilly. But the conversation with George had made it all clear to me. I was the only cat clever enough to take care of Harold. Oh no, no no. This could not be happening. But what could I do?

'There's something else, as well, Dad,' George said, interrupting my thoughts. There was no way I could tell him this.

'What? I hope nothing's wrong.' I had enough to deal with right now. Like being given away.

'No, but you know since Harold came out of hospital we've both been a bit worried about the people who are lonely.'

'Right and you and Harold have discussed this have you?' I tried to hide the fear I was feeling and have a normal conversation. I had to behave as if everything was alright in front of George although I felt sick.

'In our own way we have. And we've come up with an idea. In fact Harold and me came up with an idea to start a Sunday Lunch Club.'

'A Sunday Lunch Club?'

'Yes, we discussed the idea at length, but for someone who is always happy to tell people off, he's a bit nervous about sharing the idea with anyone else.'

'Go on.' I was intrigued. And I needed the distraction from my own problem.

'He wants us to introduce friends to the old people who don't have anyone else, and organise a lunch once a week. Or maybe once every two weeks, and then he also said maybe once a month we all go to the restaurant together like we did at Christmas last year.'

Last Christmas there'd been a power cut in Edgar Road, and we were lucky that Tomasz and Franceska were able to host those who might have been without any power to have Christmas lunch at the restaurant. There was a lovely sense of community there, among all cats and humans alike.

'I think that is a brilliant idea,' I said. 'George, well done, you and Harold have done a pretty sterling job.' It was a great idea, and I would have been jumping fully on board if I was fretting so much about my own future.

'But we need to encourage him to tell Claire or Marcus or someone, because he feels too scared to do so and without them involved it's not going to happen.'

'We'll give it some thought,' I suggested. Thinking that it was far too soon for me to have to come up with yet another plan. I was all planned out for the moment. Also, I now needed a plan so I wouldn't have to live at Harold's. Oh this was not good. It was the opposite of good.

'Maybe Harold's new cat can help too,' George suggested. I felt sick. I loved Harold, yes, but I didn't want to leave George.

'Maybe,' was all I could manage.

'Let's hope they get one who is very clever indeed then,' George finished.

I was busy worrying about how I would tell the humans that their idea to give me to Harold was not going to work when Claire announced we were all going to Harold's together.

'Meow,' I said, giving her my most loving look. How could she think of giving me away?

'You'll love this surprise, Alfie,' she said. No, no I wouldn't. Although I had figured out what was going on, I was still trying to process it and come up with a way to make sure it didn't happen.

'We're going to meet the new cat, I bet,' George said excitedly. You've already met him, I wanted to say but I couldn't. I had no idea yet how George was going to cope, because I wasn't coping.

George and I had a light lunch which felt like my last supper. I know it sounded a bit dramatic, as Harold was on the same street, but George needed me to live with him, and what about Toby and Summer? Not to mention Jonathan and Claire. Their lives would literally fall apart without me. How could they do this to me?

'If I'm going to meet a new cat, I need to make a good

impression,' George said, as he gave himself a thorough grooming.

'Is Hana coming with us?' I asked. I thought if he had his best friend there it might make things easier for him.

'She is not. She said it's too cold, and she doesn't know anything about the new cat either. I hope the new cat isn't going to have a nervous disposition, it wouldn't cope well in our family, or on Edgar Road for that matter.' George chatted away but his words barely registered with me.

Claire led George and me out of the house and to Harold's. She left the children with Polly. Of course she did, she was giving me away, and she wouldn't want them to be a party to that! I was suddenly angry. After all I had done for this family, how could they do this to me?

'Do I look alright?' George asked, as we stood at the door. I was pleased that I had taught George to always look his best as I tried to focus on him and not me for a moment.

'You are the most handsome kitten,' I replied, affectionately. Deep down I wanted to yowl but I had to pull myself together.

'Although I am NOT a kitten,' he replied, but he nuzzled me to show he didn't mind.

Claire used her key to open the door, and George rushed in to see this new cat, but Harold was sat with Marcus in the living room and they were alone. My worst fear was confirmed. There was no new cat, I was the new cat. Although George looked under the furniture just in case. No, no new cat here.

'Alfie, George, you two have been my friends for ages, especially George,' Harold said, as he sat in his favourite chair. 'And I know it was your idea that I get a cat – it's a grand idea. But I don't want you to think for one minute that this new cat will replace either of you in any way.' Oh, that was strange. If I was the new cat then how could I replace myself? Was Harold just a bit confused, after all he'd been in hospital for a long time and that could confuse anyone.

'Meow.' George jumped onto Harold's lap and nuzzled into his neck. I thought it showed how far George had come recently as he showed no sign of jealousy.

Claire looked at her watch.

'They should be here by now,' she said. 'I just can't wait.'

'Meow?' I asked, enough was enough, I needed to know. Who should be here by now? Just what on earth was going on? I yowled at Claire, begging her to tell me.

'Jonathan and Matt went to get Harold's new cat,' Claire explained to me. 'And they will be home any minute now, so get ready to give a warm welcome to her.'

Relief flooded my fur, I was not the new/old cat. I wasn't being given to Harold, and the fear I'd held the last few days was unfounded. In fact I felt a little bit silly.

But what had all the hushed conversations been about? Why was there such a big fuss being made of this? Claire was jittery, Harold excited and Marcus grinned. No, this still made no sense.

'It's going to be the best surprise ever, Alfie,' Claire said. No, no idea what she was talking about.

'I still can't get over how you guys talk to your cat as if they're human. Sylvie does too and Connie sometimes talks to Hana in Japanese if she doesn't want us to know what she's saying,' Marcus laughed.

'Since meeting George, and then Alfie, I've learnt that

these cats understand everything. I've never met a better listener than George,' Harold said.

'Meow.' George thanked him.

It seemed like a long time, all this waiting. I hopped from paw to paw, impatiently, while George and Harold sat there quietly. I still couldn't get over why they were making such a meal of this? And if Claire had told me in the first place I wouldn't have had to worry about being given away.

I was just about to start getting bored, when the doorbell went. Claire jumped up and went to the door. Matt and Jonathan came in, Marcus was stood up, and Harold levered himself up to standing.

'Everything OK?' Claire asked.

'Yes, all great. I mean sad, it was sad seeing them have to say goodbye but at least this is the best possible outcome under the circumstances,' Jonathan said, which flummoxed me even more.

Matt put the cat carrier down on the floor. He bent down to open the door. George went up to it, and finally the cat moved and stretched, but I couldn't see it. I spotted one white paw and I felt my body start to shake, as the cat began to make its way out of the cat carrier. I would never forget that paw, that scent. Suddenly all the secrets, all the hushed conversations made sense. It was never me, but it was all about me.

'Meow, meow, meow,' George said excitedly. He had no idea, as Harold's new cat emerged from the cat carrier and I found myself face to face with Snowball.

We both stared at each other. I felt as if I was glued to the carpet, as my legs continued to shake. All those feelings

I had once felt began to flood back. In front of me was my first love and she looked exactly the same. A little older maybe, but her white fur was still the fluffiest I'd ever seen and her blue eyes were mesmerising. What on earth was she doing here?

George searched my face questioningly. He had never met Snowball, he had no idea what she looked like. And I had a feeling that he wasn't going to be pleased when he discovered just who Harold's new cat was. Because of Tiger, I mean.

'Welcome to my house, Snowball,' Harold said, picking her up and stroking her. George's eyes widened and then he looked at me. The pilchard finally dropped.

'It was a bit heartbreaking,' Jonathan said. 'They are really going to miss her but at least they know she's going to a good home and of course a familiar street with friends,' he added. 'With Alfie. They were so pleased that these two were being reunited,' he added. And I would be too, if it wasn't for George.

'Oh Snowball, please don't be sad, we'll be great company for each other and you have your old friend Alfie here too,' Harold said, petting her. She snuggled into him. I guess she had accepted the move with her usual grace.

'Snowball's family, Tim and Karen Snell, are moving overseas,' Claire explained. Although to who I wasn't sure, it seemed only George and I were in the dark on this one. 'And it wasn't suitable for her to go with them, so when they told me and I mentioned that we were looking for a cat, it all fell into place.'

'I still can't believe you told them we were looking for a cat the exact time they were looking for a family for Snowball,' Marcus said. 'It's like it was fate,' he added.

'That's what I said,' Claire said, excitedly. 'Snowball and Alfie were inseparable before they moved away, he was so devastated when she left,' she added. George did not look best pleased.

'And I'm very pleased to meet you,' Harold said. 'You really are gorgeous.' He sounded delighted, but I was still trying to process all the information, and there was so much to figure out. Snowball seemed a little less shocked than me, but when Jonathan and Matt turned up she would have known what was going on, and her family had probably explained it to her, but I had a feeling she'd miss them. She had lived with them since she was a kitten and that broke my heart. However, it seemed that their loss was our gain.

I had a million questions but seeing the thunderous look on George's face, I realised he had too.

Snowball and I were trying not to look at each other. George was ignoring me. The humans were all making a massive fuss of Snowball and all I wanted to do was to speak to her alone.

'We've even got a cat flap for you,' Harold said, 'so you can come and go as you please.' He was clearly smitten but then Snowball had that effect on people, and cats actually. I tried to get George's attention – he was sulking under a chair, clearly not himself.

I took a breath. I needed to speak to Snowball, I needed to know what happened and if she was alright. I couldn't tell from her impenetrable gaze which she had trained on Harold right now. I also needed to talk to George, because of all the questions I was sure he wanted to ask. But at the moment we were stuck here, in the most awkward welcome party known to cats.

It felt so strange, all those years apart and I could still read her. It was, in some ways, like she'd never been away. My unwarranted fear of being given to Harold was replaced with a new fear. And that was that George would never accept Snowball. Claire said to Jonathan that she was surprised by our reactions, she thought we'd both be so happy to see each other, but of course I couldn't explain that to her. How could I expect a human to understand the complexities of a cat relationship?

George and I broke away from the others on the way home and went to the park at the end of Edgar Road.

'How are you feeling?' I asked, accepting how inadequate my words were. We were crouched behind a bush together, George was angrily swiping at leaves.

'I don't know,' George said sadly. 'They said Snowball was your girlfriend?'

'I know and, George, I was just as shocked as you were to see her,' I said.

'But, Dad, she can't replace Tiger,' he said. I supposed I should be grateful for him getting straight to the point.

'Of course not, George, and you can't think of her like that. We were together before Tiger and I were, when your mum and I were just friends, but I don't want you to worry about that. We haven't even had the chance to say hello properly yet,' I pointed out.

'I was excited for Harold to get a cat and I thought we'd all be best friends but now I don't know how I can be friends with her, it feels like I would be betraying Tiger mum,' he said. He looked pretty forlorn.

'And I understand that. You must feel incredibly confused, and I know I do too. But Snowball is here because she lost

270

her family, or was about to lose them, and because we persuaded our families that Harold needed a cat. We need to remember that.'

'But, I can't ignore the fact that she and you have history, and that makes me feel funny,' he said.

'I understand, George, I do, but I don't have the first clue what to say to you. Snowball will never replace Tiger in my heart. I need you to know that. We're different cats now, we're older and hopefully wiser . . .' While I was trying to reassure George, I was also trying to reassure myself, or at least organise my emotions.

'But you might love her like you used to.'

'I honestly don't know how to answer that at the moment. George, please understand me when I say that I won't do anything to hurt you and I would never ever do anything to tarnish my feelings for Tiger.'

'I hope that's true and I hope you know that I am going to have to tell Snowball that she can never be my mum.' He was getting riled now.

'You don't need to say that because she never would try to do anything like that. George, remember when Oliver moved into the Barkers' house, and I felt funny about that? You said that the Barkers needed him because they were lost without Tiger and mentioned that Oliver needed a home. Well Harold needs Snowball and Snowball needs Harold by the sounds of it and if you can be friends with Oliver, then you can be friends with Snowball surely.'

'No, because Oliver was never your girlfriend, and didn't try to replace my mum. Anyway I can't talk about this anymore right now, I'm going to go and see Hana.'

There was nothing I could do as I watched him stalk off.

My heart felt heavy as I went home. I thought about going back to see Snowball but then I realised I needed a bit of time alone.

I crept into the house and into my bed. I fell asleep and tried not to think but after about only forty blinks, I woke up, everything felt unsettled. I decided that it was time to bite the bullet, because I wouldn't settle until I had a proper chat with Snowball. I needed to know she was alright. So I made my way back to Harold's house, hoping George was happily with Hana and didn't get mad at me if he found out. I had no idea how to do the right thing. Firstly I had to worry about George's feelings, then Snowball's and finally my own.

I let myself in the cat flap and found Snowball in the living room sitting on Harold's lap. He was asleep. It was strange, seeing her evoked myriad emotions. In some ways they looked as if they belonged together and had been together for years, they seemed so comfortable. Yet, also I couldn't help but remember how much pain I had been in when I said goodbye to her years ago, and how much had happened since. I'd become a father – albeit initially reluctantly – I'd fallen in love with Tiger, I'd been on holiday a number of times, we'd met Harold, there was almost a whole life between when I last saw her and now. And I was a very different cat from the one who tried to woo her by climbing a tree with dug up flowers. That had ended in me getting rescued by the fire brigade and was so humiliating, by the way. I would never do that now! Especially as that was how I discovered my fear of heights.

Snowball peered at me and I thought 'I still know you.'

It was in her eyes. I tilted my head and hoped that she would follow me as I made my way to the back door.

'He sleeps very soundly,' I said. It was the first thing I'd said to her and it was horribly inadequate.

'He snores loudly,' she replied with a grin.

'Where do we start, Snowball?' I asked.

'At the beginning?' she replied.

'Tell me, because Claire was vague, why you're here. Your family moved away?' I wanted to nuzzle her but it felt too soon for that sort of contact.

'The kids moved away ages ago, and somehow they both ended up in America. So, they all missed each other and Tim and Karen decided to move, but they couldn't really take me, because where they were moving to would be too hot. They said at my age it would probably be best for me to stay here.'

'That must have been devastating for you?'

'I kind of got used to losing people, Alfie. First you, then Daisy moved away to be a model, then Christopher left home . . . I miss everyone, of course, and when I found out Tim and Karen were moving I was utterly heartbroken. But then they spoke to Claire and told me I'd be coming back to Edgar Road, and although I was still sad, I thought about you and how no matter what the situation was with us, we'd be friends again. I felt a bit better, because I didn't have to start over from scratch. But then when I saw you this afternoon, it was so strange. And I don't think George liked me. Oh, Alfie, it's all so confusing.'

'Let me fill you in on what's been going on here since you've been gone,' I said, trying to find a starting point for this new situation between us both.

We talked for what felt like hours. I told her about how heartbroken I was when she left, and how my family thought the answer lay in giving me George as a kitten. I then told her about how we got to know each other and how in doing so, Tiger became even closer to me. I told her about our adventures and finally I got onto losing Tiger, and the new cat who was living in her old house. I filled her in on so much, it was quite tiring for me, talking so much.

In turn, she told me about how after she moved from Edgar Road, she had a very different life. They lived in a house with a garden on a street which was smaller than Edgar Road, and there weren't many cats around and so, unlike me, Snowball had been living quite a quiet and solitary existence since leaving here. Well that was at an end now she was back here.

'You do realise that life on Edgar Road is still not remotely peaceful or quiet,' I said.

'I do, and if I remember rightly, life with you is never dull,' Snowball said and I saw another glimpse of the girl I left behind.

'You know when life is calm and quiet, I always start to panic that it's going to change drastically. It always happens; this time everything was alright then Pickles arrived in our lives. Shortly after Harold went to hospital, George got a job, then Sylvie found out she was pregnant and now here you are. I mean dull? I don't even know the meaning of the word dull.'

'Oh, Alfie, there is so much we need to catch up on,' Snowball said. 'Where do we go from here?'

'Do you think we can start to rebuild our friendship now? See, what happens?' I asked.

'I think that's the best way. We need to think about George. I mean he seemed pretty angry.'

'He's confused. He thinks you're going to replace Tiger, and we have to prove to him that that's not the case. No matter what happens between the two of us, we have to make George feel good about the situation first off, because he and Harold are so close. And he's my son, my number one priority.'

'OK, so, Alfie, I've been here five minutes and you're already going to have to come up with one of your crazy plans.'

'Hey.' I bumped her gently, old feelings began to come flooding back again. 'My plans are not crazy.'

We turned and grinned at each other and I knew that although I had lived a life without her in it, I still adored her. It wasn't the same as I felt with Tiger, but I needed to figure out how to go from here. Snowball and I agreed that George was the first priority here, the rest would have to wait.

Chapter
Twenty-Seven

I knew George was stubborn but boy was he stubborn.

'You can't decide you're not visiting Harold anymore because of Snowball, he's your best friend,' I said. That was my first part of the plan, trying to encourage George to get to know Snowball via Harold. That way they could become friends, without me being there. That was the idea, anyway.

'Harold doesn't need me, he's got her,' he said. It wasn't going well.

'You know that's not true, we talked about jealousy, George, and it doesn't work. And not only that but it's not fair on Harold. He loves you and he's done nothing wrong.' I should have pointed out that none of us had done anything wrong actually but I was taking baby steps.

'I'm sure you're there all the time anyway, no one needs me, anymore,' George whined.

'I need you,' Pickles said, but George wasn't remotely placated by his comment.

'George, Snowball only moved in just over a week ago and we've only spoken briefly and that was because I wanted to tell her about you. Everyone needs you, me most of all, but also Harold.' It was exasperating.

'Hmmph,' he said.

'George, you have to see that Snowball didn't come here on purpose, she had no choice. She's lost her family, she's alone, and she's not here to replace Tiger.'

'I don't want her here, you loved her before you loved Tiger mum, and I don't like that.'

'George, if Tiger was still here, then we'd be having this conversation and I would tell you that I would never leave Tiger for Snowball, but she's not here, and I'm alone in that way. I'm not saying that Snowball will be my girlfriend again, but she is here now and whatever happens I have to find a way to make you OK with that. Because you're my priority.'

'Hmmph.'

'Right, I am going to visit Harold and Snowball, are you coming?'

'No. I have to see Hana.'

'Can I come?' Pickles asked, hopefully.

'No,' both George and I said at the same time. I felt guilty.

'Pickles, Claire is going to be cross if you go out and I really do need to but I promise I won't be long and if you stay here and are good, then I'll play with you when I get back.'

'Promise?' He looked at me with his big eyes.

'Promise,' I said, wearily.

It was beyond frustrating. I went alone to see Snowball who was settling in well, despite the fact she missed her family terribly. But Harold had taken to her, he seemed to adore her already, although of course it was very early days.

'So where's George?' Harold asked, as he fussed me. He then put down some food for us. I bet George would be missing eating his biscuits dunked in tea with Harold. I would remind him of that.

'Meow,' I replied. I would tell George later how Harold was missing him, I would go on and on until George relented and went to see him.

Snowball and I sat in the back garden.

'I can't wait to see the others. Do you think Harold will mind if I go out for a bit?' I knew that Marcus was coming round, because Harold told me, so I thought that we'd be alright to go out. As Snowball had lived on Edgar Road before, it felt unnecessary to keep her in like they did with new cats sometimes. Also she had me to escort her, so I took the opportunity to take Snowball to see our friends. It would be a reunion of sorts.

'Hi, guys,' I said, 'look who's back.'

'Oh my goodness,' Nellie said, nuzzling Snowball. Elvis and Rocky crowded round. 'Thank goodness you're back, what a turn up for the books. I've been moaning that I don't have any female company as well.'

'I have no idea who you are, but it's nice to meet you,' Oliver said. We all started talking at once. It was like the old days, but of course without Tiger, and I felt almost happy again, actually, genuinely happy. Then a voice interrupted us.

'So now she's muscled her way in with all of you,' George stormed. We all sprang apart and faced George who was angrier than I've ever seen him.

'George, this isn't like you,' Nellie said. 'Snowball is an old friend.'

'Can't you see what she's trying to do? She's trying to replace Tiger,' George persisted.

Our cat friends looked shocked, and Snowball appeared devastated as she scrunched up her lovely face.

'No, George, no I'm not,' she said quietly. 'But I've lost everyone I cared about and now I'm here and I'm with old friends. And new ones I hope, but that's all it is.' She turned to walk away. I was horrified, sad and worried all at the same time, but more than anything I was angry. I had not brought George up to be like this.

'George, that was rude, and you are going to come with me and we're going to sort this out once and for all,' I shouted.

'Go, lad,' Rocky said. 'We love you and we loved Tiger but Snowball was our friend too,' he said, quietly. I was grateful for his support.

'Come on,' I said again and set off, I turned and thankfully George was following me. We caught up with Snowball. 'Let's go to mutual ground,' I said. And the three of us headed to the park.

George sulked the whole way there so Snowball and I remained silent. We arrived at the entrance to the park and headed to one of George's favourite places, where there was a big climbable tree.

'So,' I started, 'Harold is missing you. He really wants to see you and I know you're missing him too.'

'Not my fault,' he replied. I paused, a little unsure where to go next.

'George,' Snowball said, gently. 'Perhaps it's time you told me what your problem with me is because I am not trying to replace Tiger. Gosh, I could never replace Tiger,' she added.

'I just don't like you,' George said, sounding more like a kitten than he was.

'You don't know her, son,' I pointed out.

'But I know you were my dad's girlfriend once and now you're back again and I just don't like it.'

'OK, I understand that, but, George, if we're going to get

past this, we need to talk. I have no choice but to live with Harold. Don't forget that Harold loves you.'

'But I feel sad. Because of Tiger mum, I loved her so much, and I miss her,' he mumbled.

'Oh, George, I know, and your dad misses her too, and all the friends I just saw. Tiger was a wonderful cat, and we were friends, your mum and me, you know.'

'Really?' George didn't sound convinced.

'Although actually you and Tiger have something in common talking of not liking me,' Snowball said, with a grin.

'What?' George couldn't help but sound curious.

'She didn't like me either at first,' Snowball said.

'She really didn't,' I added.

'Really? Why didn't she like you?'

'Pretty much the same reason as you don't like me, because of me and your dad.'

'But she came to like you?'

'Yes, we ended up as great friends. She was a wonderful cat.' Snowball stood up. 'George, do you like climbing trees?'

'I love it,' he said, as he softened to her.

'Why don't the two of us go and climb a tree? I can tell you about the time your dad ended up stuck up a tree in my garden.'

George blinked and then tilted his head to one side as if he was thinking. He had heard the story before of course but not from Snowball.

'OK, and then I'll decide if I like you. But you can't make me.'

'Wouldn't dream of it.' Snowball grinned and I realised that no one, not even George would be able to resist her for long.

I watched them go off together and they started climbing.
I had to stop watching when they got a bit high, because it
made me feel funny. My vertigo could kick in even if I was
on the ground, it seemed.

I huddled under a bush to keep warm while I waited for
them, paws crossed they would come down friends.

They were quiet when they came to find me, which could
have meant anything. I stood up and stretched.

'All OK?'

'I have decided to be mature and give Snowball a chance.
After all it's not her fault that she had to come back to Edgar
Road and like Oliver she's lost her family, although she didn't
go to the shelter, so we need to be kind and thoughtful about
that. And I do miss Harold. And biscuits dunked in tea.'

'George, you never cease to surprise me with your maturity,' I said. Apart from when he was immature of course but
I didn't voice that.

'And I have promised I won't try to replace Tiger, not that
I ever could, but we can all be friends now,' Snowball said.

'And I need to see Harold immediately to make sure he
knows I still care about him,' he said. 'That was bad of me,
none of this was Harold's fault, or Snowball's actually. Are
you coming, Dad?'

I looked at them both, my first love and my favourite cat
in the world, my son, and I was so relieved they were getting
along. I realised I didn't need to be there after all.

'How about the two of you go and you can continue to
get to know each other,' I suggested.

'Aren't you worried I might tell more stories about you?'
Snowball asked, with a grin.

'No.' I swished my tail. 'I think the fire brigade rescue was my most humiliating moment.'

'There was also the time you fell in cow poo,' she added. Oh no, I'd forgotten about that.

'Oh you must tell me about that, come on, Snowball, I need to go and see Harold right this minute.'

They trotted off and I felt my heart swell again, I was pretty sure that all would be alright, but I would have to be careful, because George needed to continue to feel secure. That was my priority. I didn't know how I felt about Snowball at this stage, I remembered all my romantic feelings, they had all returned, but I also knew we were both different cats now. A lot of water had passed under the bridge, and it felt as if we needed to get to know each other again. Which both scared and excited me. But there was plenty of time, I knew that, and I also knew that whatever I did, however I moved forward I would always respect Tiger and also respect George's feelings. But I also recognised how seeing Snowball again had been a little like a reawakening for me.

I was always so busy worrying about other people and their feelings that I didn't have much time for my own. When I saw Oliver at the Barkers', it hit home how much I missed having companionship, so when I saw Snowball and felt how wonderful seeing her made me feel, I realised I was still very much alive, and it was time for me to start living.

Chapter
Twenty-Eight

Chapter
Twenty-Eight

George had agreed to give Snowball a chance, although I felt I should give Snowball a bit of a wide berth for the moment while things were still tender between them.

The children were out with Jonathan and Matt. Pickles was in his bed, George was either with Hana or Harold and Snowball. Claire and I were enjoying the peace and quiet when the doorbell rang. I went with Claire to answer the door and was pleased to see Aleksy on the doorstep, on his own.

'Hey, Alfie, Claire,' he said as he came in. He leant down to pet me. Pickles, who had been asleep, appeared.

'Woof, woof, woof,' he said, licking Aleksy's leg.

'Ughh, Pickles you are a rubbish guard dog.' He picked him up and petted him as Pickles licked his face. 'I hear Snowball's back, I can't wait to see her,' he said.

'You should go and see her, take Connie as well,' Claire said.

'I think we're going in a bit.'

'Woof!'

'Can I take Pickles?' Aleksy said.

'If you promise not to let him off the lead.'

'Woof.' Pickles licked his face again. That dog could get his way with anything, it seemed.

'Right, Aleksy, it's nice to see you but what do I owe the pleasure?' Claire asked.

'I want to buy a present for Connie, you know for Christmas,' he said, blushing. 'She's going to Japan, which means I won't see her on Christmas Day, but I want to tell her that I care and also make her feel as if I'm OK about her going.'

'You couldn't ask your mum?' Claire asked.

'No, she'll only tell me to buy her one of those funny neck pillows to use on the plane.' She did; Franceska was known to only spend money on things that she deemed useful.

'So what were you thinking?' Claire asked. She was smiling and I think she found it sweet, as did I, that Aleksy had come to her for help.

'Jewellery, I heard women like that,' he said looking at his feet.

'They certainly do.' Claire smiled. 'So why me?'

'Because you have good taste and Jonathan says that shopping is the thing you do best,' Aleksy replied. Claire rolled her eyes. Jonathan did say that. A lot.

'Right, come with me, we'll hit the internet,' Claire said and they went to the kitchen to her laptop.

'Is the internet something I can eat?' Pickles asked me.

'No, it is not and you need to stop trying to eat everything,' I chastised.

'OK, Alfie,' he replied as he licked me.

I decided, that I'd go and see my friends while Aleksy took Pickles. I hadn't seen much of them since Snowball was back, because as I said before, I was still processing my feelings. I headed out into the cold, shivering as I first hit the outdoors, and made my way down. I was disappointed to find no one was there but it was a freezing day, so it was also understandable. I stayed for a bit, wondering whether to head back when I spotted George walking down the road.

'Hey,' I shouted and went to join him.

'Why haven't you been to Harold's for a while?' he asked as we fell into step with each other.

'I just wanted to give you the chance to spend time with Harold. Your old dad can give you some space you know. So how are you finding it?'

'Dad, I know I was upset at first but you have to admit that it is strange that your old girlfriend turns up, but I actually like her. I really like her, she's funny, and I like that she's nothing like Tiger mum as well. Although Tiger mum was funny, she and Snowball are very different. You really don't have a type do you?'

'No,' I laughed. 'I don't have a type. But I also have a lot of feelings—'

'I do know, and I don't want to talk about that but there is something I do want to talk about.'

'Right, go on?'

'It's about Harold's idea for the Sunday Lunch Club. He's got a list of people who don't have anyone and he's even written it all down in a notebook. I chatted about it with Snowball as well and we both think that it'll be great for our community if we could put it into practice.'

'Right, so you guys now have your own little plan, seeing as you wouldn't talk to her a few days ago that's interesting,' I teased.

'Stop it, Dad. But you know my job, it's not at the hospital anymore, but I still have it. I still have to try to help lonely people you know.'

'I know and I'm proud of you.'

'But we need your help,' George said.

I felt as if we had come so far. I was so delighted that George and Snowball were actually in cohorts about something, I was pleased Harold was doing something as well, but I didn't know where we went from here.

'My help with what?'

'Harold is too nervous about his idea to tell any humans, is there a way we can put it in practice on our own?'

As much as I was a cat who normally put plans into action, arranging for people to cook for other people and take care of them was possibly beyond me. It definitely needed human intervention.

'We need one of them to hear the idea, so we need to encourage Harold to tell them,' I said.

'But how do we do that? I mean he's happy to talk to Snowball and me but that's as far as it goes,' George said.

'Then we need to find a way to get him to tell the others, and they can help get it set up, I know they can,' I said.

'But how?' George asked.

'George, I think we need another plan.'

'I was hoping you'd say that. But I also think we need Snowball's input on this one.'

'Really?' It seemed she had won my boy over.

'Yes, she told me about your past, and some of your plans have been really terrible. With her help, I reckon we can keep us all out of danger.'

I had no words.

'It's a bit like old times isn't it?' Snowball asked as we sat in Harold's garden discussing what George had told me earlier.

'Different house but yes,' I replied, feeling a mixture of

nostalgia and confusion. I felt warm despite the fact it was freezing and being next to Snowball was making me happy.

'Alfie, I feel that I've bonded with George, but I also think it all hinges on his plan. If we can't get Harold to tell the others about the Sunday Lunch Club, George will be so disappointed and I can't bear to let him down.'

'I agree, I want to make it happen too, not least because I love that he accepted you so quickly.'

'It wasn't that quick, he froze me out for over a week.'

'Believe me, for George that's nothing. He didn't talk to me for ages not that long ago. Anyway, any ideas about how to get Harold to tell the others? I really don't know why he won't.'

'He says he thinks they might just say he's a silly old man and not take it seriously,' Snowball told me. 'It's totally irrational because it's a great idea, but he doesn't seem to have confidence in himself.'

'Poor Harold, not only is it brilliant, but he's given it a lot of thought, according to George.'

'Weirdly he swears that he and George came up with the idea together, I have no idea how that worked though,' Snowball said.

'You said he'd written it down?'

'Yes, he's got this notebook and he said the other day he'd made a list of people and also written a bit about how his idea would work.'

'Where is this notebook?' I asked.

'He leaves it on the arm of his chair, mostly,' she replied. 'Why?'

'I think I might have an idea . . .'

'Just like old times.'

'What did you think of Pickles?' I asked. I hadn't seen him since he'd been to Snowball's house. I think Aleksy must have taken him back to Polly's.

'Interesting little fellow. Kept trying to lick me,' Snowball replied.

'You better get used to that. Did you fall in love, when you moved away?' I hadn't asked this question directly yet.

'No, I didn't. But I know about you and Tiger. She always loved you.'

'And I grew to love her, but it was different than with you, not better, not worse, not more or less, just different.'

'I do understand. I did feel a bit jealous at first, but then that's natural.'

'Yes, and you will always be my first love, Snowball. Remember how hard I had to work to woo you.' We both laughed.

'It's strange, I'm still upset about my family, I know they had to move and I know they thought long and hard about taking me with them, but . . .'

'Snowball, it was only when Claire told them that we were looking for a cat that they actually made up their minds, because you know their reasons.'

'I know, and I don't like the heat – I'm much more a winter cat.'

'You live up to your name,' I joked.

'And settling in with Harold is very strange. He's lovely, don't get me wrong but it's the two of us so much of the time and the others were out of the house a lot whereas Harold isn't, so I do have more company. And he's a lovely man and seeing you again, and my other friends and meeting George . . .'

'It's not all bad is it?'

'No, it's not bad at all.' Then Snowball snuggled into me a bit and we sat there like that in silence. In that moment, I realised that you can love lots of people, because I realised that I absolutely still loved her.

Chapter
Twenty-Nine

He wasn't the most obvious love guru but since he'd been spending time with Ally, Dustbin had definitely changed. He'd softened slightly and he was definitely happier. He had more of a spring in his step. That's what love did to you. And I had a spring in my step that cold, frosty December morning when I went to see him. I needed some clarity and I think I needed it away from Edgar Road. I had left George in sole charge of Pickles, because I had done more than my fair share of Pickles sitting. George said he was happy to do that and he had gone off to get Hana to come round to ours too to keep them both company. She'd agreed, of course, being the most agreeable cat ever. In order to get away I told him I was working on the plan to get Harold's 'lonely people club', which is what George had named it, up and running. And I was working on that but I was also working on myself. Because there was a part of my heart which did feel lonely, I could acknowledge that now.

When Snowball moved away, I didn't even want pilchards, that was how bad my heartbreak was. But then Claire had come up with the genius plan to get George, and although I loved him more than anyone I'd ever loved, because he was my son, the part of my heart reserved for a different love had been empty. After Tiger, I hadn't considered ever falling in love again. I was confused. I felt guilty. For George, for Tiger, and for Snowball. I wasn't in the habit of just falling in love all over the place, there had only been two loves in my life after all. Claire said it was fate, and although Jonathan didn't believe in fate, maybe I did.

My thoughts had brought me all the way to Dustbin's yard.

'I wasn't expecting to see you, Alfie,' he said.

'I needed someone to talk to,' I replied and I told him how I was feeling. 'I still love Snowball, my old feelings have come back as strong as ever but I don't know what to do because of George?'

'You know George has been through a tough time, which is why he reacted so badly to having Snowball back,' Dustbin said, when I explained all. 'Understandable but he did get over that quite quickly. He might not like the idea of the two of you together but I think he'll come round. He's a clever cat.'

'I know, but I don't want to hurt anyone.'

'Ah, yes, but you know all Tiger really cared about was your happiness, I am sure she still cares about that. Tiger is gone, which is horrible, and you'll never forget her. The problem is, Alfie, life moves on and you have to move with it.'

'You're so wise,' I said. I was feeling so sad that I lay down and let myself have a little yowl.

'And we both know that life doesn't last forever, so we have to live it to the fullest. When I met Ally, I wasn't interested in companionship. You know me, I'm only friends with you because you were so persistent, didn't give me much choice, and I'm glad I am. And it was thanks to you that I was able to open my heart up to Ally too. You're a good friend, Alfie, no, the best friend a cat could have, and that being said, you deserve to be happy too.'

'Love and friendship, that's all we want isn't it?'

'Two important things and you taught me them.'

'And about the joys of pilchards! In fact, I really fancy some pilchards.'

'Shall we go to the restaurant door, look hungry and see if they'll find something for us?' Dustbin smiled.

'You're speaking my language.'

As we ate sardines, not pilchards, but I'm not one to complain, Dustbin and I discussed the idea Harold had for his lonely people.

'Remember last Christmas, when you got everyone to the restaurant. That's probably what inspired Harold.'

'You might be right. He goes to this senior centre once a week but he says that some people there don't see anyone apart from that, and often they don't have a proper cooked meal, because they only cook the basics themselves. It's sad.'

'But he's got the idea, so all you need to do is to let one of the humans find out about it.'

'Yes, I think Claire, this is right up her street, but I don't understand why Harold won't tell her about it.'

'It sounds as though he's lacking in confidence,' Dustbin pointed out.

'He told Snowball he's worried they'll think it's a silly idea and laugh it off,' I explained. Dustbin was right. Harold had lost a bit of confidence since being ill, actually, I think it worried him at times, how vulnerable he was. Although I had never suffered a lack of confidence, I could understand it.

'Right, but, Alfie, if he's written it down then all you need to do is to get one of them to read what he's written.' He said it as if it was simple, and as I thought about it, I realised that it was.

'Oh, Dustbin, you are a genius on so many levels. Of course, I'll steal the notebook and take it to Claire.' My mind was whirring again. Perhaps I wasn't as planned out as I thought.

'Or you might find it easier to take Claire to the notebook, and it might be a bit less risky,' Dustbin narrowed his eyes at me.

'Of course, Dustbin you really are the best.' I calmed down and realised he was right. I was a cat. How on earth would I carry a notebook?

'And tell George that this was your idea. You get this done for him and Harold, and then you will possibly soften him up a bit when you tell him how you feel about Snowball.'

'Since when did you become the king of plans?' I asked, only slightly affronted, because normally this was my department.

'Since your head has been full of confusion about Snowball. Don't worry you'll have the crown back in no time.' He grinned at me, and I grinned right back.

I was so happy as I walked back, things were coming together, I could feel it. My humans were happy, my cats were happy, Pickles was happy – although Pickles was always happy. I felt fully confident of being happy. But as soon as I went through the cat flap I could hear loud and upset voices, and that didn't sound very good. I immediately panicked, I had left George with Pickles; what if something had happened to either of them?

'It's my fault,' Claire was saying, 'I shouldn't have been so stupid.'

'Claire, calm down, you're not stupid,' Sylvie said, hugging Claire. Polly had our cat carrier in her arms, which she put down on the floor.

'Claire, of course kids leave chocolate lying around at

302

Christmas, it happens, and I'll get him straight to the vet, honestly, it could have happened at our house.'

I wondered what was going on but Pickles was lying on the floor, a snorting noise coming out of his mouth, his eyes were droopy, he had a sort of white foam and he didn't look like his normal self at all. I felt panic in the tips of my fur. What was wrong with Pickles? He hadn't even moved since I got home. George was sitting watching with a horrified look on his face. I turned to him.

'What happened?' I asked, as Polly grabbed Pickles and managed to get him into our carrier.

'It wasn't my fault,' George said, eyes wide.

'I'm sure it wasn't. But what wasn't?'

'Pickles ate some chocolate coins that he found in the living room, where the kids had them, and apparently dogs are allergic to chocolate so now he has to go to the vet, but he just said how much he liked them, even the foil they were wrapped in.'

'He ate the foil?'

'Some of it. Dad, I told him not to eat them but he didn't listen.'

'Did you tell him that cats never eat chocolate?'

'No, I didn't think of that. I'll tell him that later, if he's alright. Do you think he'll be alright? Oh, Dad, he has to be alright.'

'He's going to the vet, he'll be in good hands, like Harold was at the hospital. I'm sure he'll be fine.' I wasn't sure at all, I thought, as I watched Polly lift him gently into the car carrier.

'I realised that I love him, Dad,' George said, his eyes sad.

'We all do, son, we all do.'

I put all thoughts of my plan aside as I tried to console

George. He wasn't going anywhere until he knew that Pickles was alright, he was more fond of the puppy than he let on. He also felt guilty and no matter how many times I told him it wasn't his fault, he didn't believe me.

'And Hana had only just left, you see I was saying goodbye to her at the back door and I came back in and he was already eating them. I only turned my back for a minute.'

'George, Pickles eats anything and everything, there is just no stopping him.' It was true, even I wouldn't want to come between that dog and his food. Or anyone else's food for that matter.

While we waited for news, Claire was beside herself, as were we all. It was as if we all blamed ourselves, although I wasn't there I still felt as if I was responsible in some way. We fretted and paced around, restless, hoping that the poor pup would be alright. George lay down eventually, but I knew he wasn't able to sleep, so I lay next to him nuzzling him, trying to offer some comfort.

Finally, Polly rang with the news that Pickles was going to be alright, although he was still a bit sick. Pickles was going to stay with the vet for a while, for something called observation, and then he'd be home before we knew it. Claire was relieved, although no one blamed her for it, she blamed herself, a bit like George. Claire cried while I comforted her, it hadn't been fun that was for sure.

But when we knew that Pickles was going to be alright, I persuaded George to go and visit Harold and Snowball.

'Are you going to come with me?'

'No, son, I'm exhausted and need to rest,' I said. I had a plan in place that Dustbin had come up with about the notebook, but for now I had another plan, one of my own. I was hoping the more George and Snowball bonded, the easier it would be when I told him how I felt about her. That was my biggest wish right now. Of course I had to tell Snowball too but I thought that it was almost understood between us already, without us having to say anything. But George was the one whose feelings I had to consider most at the moment, I was a parent after all and his feelings were more important than my own.

When George came home that evening, I had slept, and thought, slept and thought some more. Because of everything going around my brain, I was still tired though.

'How were Harold and Snowball?' I asked.

'I forgot that Harold was at his senior centre this afternoon so I only just saw him when he came home. He was talking about his lonely club again. He's got ten people so far on his list who don't really have family around, and he's very sad about it. As am I. But I told Snowball that you had a plan coming soon.'

'I do, George, I do.'

'And on the way home I stopped at Polly's and Pickles is back, he said they made him be sick, but that he's fine now although quite hungry.'

'Ah, that puppy is always hungry.'

'I know but he wasn't bothered by it. He said it was another adventure. But I did tell him that cats would never eat chocolate or foil, and he said he had taken that onboard now. But he also said there was a lot of information in being a cat, so he wasn't sure how much he could retain.'

'That sounds like Pickles.'

'I love him, Dad, but at the end of the day he's only a dog after all.'

I went into the living room where Summer was crying. Jonathan had just got home from work and was scratching his head as if he was confused. I wished he'd scratch my head as much as he did his own, I love a good head scratch.

'Summer, what's wrong?' Claire asked.

'Henry and Martha said we had nearly killed Pickles and they're really mad at us,' Toby explained.

'They were our chocolate coins,' Summer said hiccuping the words out.

'I know, and now we know about Pickles and the fact he can't eat chocolate maybe we can be more careful about leaving it lying around. It shouldn't really have been in the living room anyway,' Claire said gently, hugging Summer. 'But it was a mistake that's all and Pickles is fine. Let's go to Polly and Matt's now and sort it out.'

'But what if they shout at us?' Toby asked.

'They must have been very worried but, Toby, Summer, this could have happened to anyone, so let's go and I'm sure it'll be fine.'

'We'll all go,' Jonathan said. 'As a family.' And off they went.

'It seems everyone feels guilty about Pickles,' George said when we were alone.

'That's what we do when we love someone, we blame ourselves if anything happens.'

'I know, you always do with me don't you?'

'Yes, George, I do.'

'But I'm perfect so you really don't need to,' he finished.

Chapter Thirty

It was time to put everything aside and get yet another plan put into action, before Christmas was upon us. After Pickles' scare, friendships between the children had been fixed and were as strong as ever, and their excitement levels had been turned up several notches. Apart from Tommy. I could tell Tommy was feeling a bit like the odd one out. Too old for the younger ones, and excluded from the exclusive Aleksy and Connie club. Franceska told Claire that she was worried he was a bit lonely. He had loads of friends but when he was with us, he wasn't really there. Claire suggested that Tommy should be allowed to invite a friend to our next family day which was coming up and that turned out to be a brilliant idea as Tommy leapt at it. Franceska said she hadn't before thought of it, as the family day was just that but our family expanded all the time. We'd added Sylvie, Connie, Hana, Marcus and Harold after all. So, this seemed like the opportune time to try to get Harold's idea to Claire.

In fact the next family day was a mini Christmas Day because Connie was spending actual Christmas in Japan. I thought that although she would be missed, it would be nice for Tommy to have his brother back for Christmas. And although Sylvie had been panicking a bit, having never spent Christmas without Connie, she had Marcus and all of us to get her through it.

I discussed the plan at length with George, and to a lesser extent with Snowball and we decided that the next time

Claire went to Harold's we would follow her there. That would be the time to get her to see the notebook. We had come up with a rough idea of how we would do it, but we also recognised the need for us to play it by ear a bit. As with most plans, they should never be too rigid. Luckily we didn't have too long to wait, Claire went to Harold's most days, so today we went with her. Claire was taking him his lunch. She was also taking Pickles who seemed to come everywhere, no one wanted to let him out of their sight since the chocolate incident. Harold always had somewhere to eat, Sylvie's, ours or Matt and Polly's, but since having Snowball he preferred to eat at home. She really had done a great job keeping him company, but I could see where Harold was coming from with his lunch club because he always had somewhere to go, or people going to see him. He was one of the lucky ones.

'Hi, Claire and Pickles,' Harold said as he answered the door. He was looking quite healthy these days. The right medication coupled with Snowball also seemed to have given him a new lease of life. 'And hello, Alfie and George. Snowball's in the kitchen,' he said. We all followed him through, including Pickles. I realised I hadn't quite factored Pickles into my plan but hopefully he wouldn't ruin it.

'Do you want some soup now? I can warm it up for you,' Claire said.

'Oh I don't want to put you to any trouble,' Harold said.

'Don't be silly, I was hoping you might invite me to join you for lunch,' Claire suggested. She was so good, she always made it sound like he was doing her a favour when really we all knew it was the other way round.

'Of course, I'd love that. I'll set the table.'

'Woof!' Pickles tried to jump up onto the chair where Harold was laying cutlery out. He was old fashioned like that. In fact, his late wife, Marcus's mum, always liked things done properly. Harold used table mats, and napkins and everything. We all sat there as Claire warmed up the soup on the stove, buttered thick slices of bread, and dished everything up.

'Pickles come here,' I hissed. I needed to keep him under control.

'You know, I can help you with your Christmas shopping if you like,' Claire offered.

'That's kind of you. Jonathan said your best skill is shopping,' Harold said.

'I'll kill him,' Claire laughed.

'But seriously, I want to get something special for Marcus and Sylvie, and young Connie. And the rest of you. I've put you all through a lot this year.'

'Oh Harold, don't think of it like that, they love you, we love you.'

'I know, but I was in hospital for a long time and you all must have been exhausted visiting me.'

'Well you know, I'll help choose for your family, but with our family we decided to do Secret Santa, not the kids, but they get loads anyway, but the adults will pick one person and you have to buy something for five pounds.'

'That sounds sensible, if you're sure. I mean I'm not a rich man but I saved quite a bit of my pension while I was in hospital.' He grinned.

'No, concentrate on your immediate family, we don't need anything but your company. Although this time next year you'll have another little one to add to your list.'

'I can't believe it, Grandpa Harold,' he chuckled. 'Now I do need to get a present for Snowball and George and Alfie, of course,' he said.

'Woof.'

'Yes and you too Pickles,' he added with a grin.

I led my troops into the kitchen and Pickles waddled in after us.

'Right, the notebook is on the arm of the chair, so my plan is that we knock it off, make a lot of noise, make sure one of us keeps a paw on it until Claire comes up to it to see what's going on.'

'Harold might get to it first,' Snowball said.

'What is this plan?' Pickles asked.

'Don't worry about it, Pickles,' Snowball said, as George shot him a withering look.

'Claire is much faster than Harold,' I reassured. 'She'll be over with us before Harold can even get off the chair.'

'It's a good plan,' George said.

'And for once one that can't end up with any of us in danger,' Snowball added. I narrowed my eyes at her, she was one cheeky cat.

'But what is the plan?' Pickles asked again.

I took the lead as I went into the living room, with them hot on my paws. I jumped up onto the armchair and then onto the arm where the notebook lay. I lifted a paw and knocked it off. George immediately pounced but somehow managed to slide it under the sofa.

'Meow,' I said. Both Harold and Claire looked over at us, but the notebook couldn't be seen. I jumped down and the three of us set about trying to catch the notebook with our paws to get it out, but we seemed to only knock it further.

'What are they doing?' Claire asked.

'Right,' I hissed quietly. 'George, you're the smallest, you have to hook it and bring it out, after all you can get under the sofa.' I held my breath, but finally the notebook emerged, followed by George who was covered in dust. He sneezed. We had done it though, now we had the notebook, I put my paw on it.

'YOWL,' I shouted.

'MEOW,' George said at the top of his lungs.

'YELP,' Snowball called out but her voice was far too sweet to be alarming.

'Woof, woof, woof,' Pickles joined in as he ran around in circles.

'What?' Harold asked as we kept making as much noise as we could. As I thought, Claire ran over to us.

'What's all the noise for?' she asked. I looked down at the notebook then back up at her.

'Meow,' I said more quietly.

'What's this?' She picked the book up. As I planned, Harold had stood up.

'That's mine,' he snapped.

'OK, but why did the cats have it?' Claire asked, as it fell open at the place where he kept his pen.

'Don't look' Harold shouted.

'Have you been writing poetry or something?' Claire asked.

'Don't be ridiculous, I just—'

'MEOW,' George shouted really loudly and jumped on Claire's foot.

'Ow. I think he wants me to read it,' she said.

'No!' Harold said.

'Meow,' the three of us said in unison.

'Why don't you want me to see it?' Claire asked. 'Of course I won't look if you don't want me to.' She handed the notebook back to Harold. I couldn't believe it, we hadn't factored in the fact that Claire wasn't an intrusive person.

'MEOW!' I shouted.

'It's just silly ramblings of an old man.' Harold blushed and looked at his feet. George jumped up on his lap and purred into his neck.

'You're not silly,' Claire said quietly. She reached over and squeezed Harold's hand which was shaking.

'Here,' was all he said, as he passed the notebook over to her.

We had succeeded, and Claire started reading as we all sat there hopefully. I noticed how Harold's hand still shook gently as he tried to eat his soup, and kept shooting glances at Claire. He was nervous, but he shouldn't have been.

'Wow,' Claire said as she finished. 'Harold, this is such a brilliant idea, why didn't you tell me?'

'You really think so?' he asked. 'I thought perhaps people would think me silly. I know I'm a foolish old man but being in hospital was a real eye-opener.'

'Goodness no, you're right we don't think enough about all the lonely people . . . Oh my goodness and you've even made a list of names.'

'It's the ones from the senior centre, they really do get very lonely and you know they don't have anyone to bring them a hot meal. It made me realise how lucky I was when I started going there and then in hospital, I had the most visitors but some people didn't have any which is why George became so important to them. I keep meaning to take him back in but of course I need help and I didn't think any of you would approve.'

'Firstly, I will help you take George to the hospital, as it's Christmas we can take biscuits and chocolates for the patients, it'll be a lovely thing to do and I only wish I'd thought of it.' Claire took Harold's hand and I saw that he had tears in his eyes. 'And as for your genius idea of the Sunday Lunch Club, how about we make it our project. We'll work together and get it off the ground straight away.'

'You mean it?'

'Yes, we're going to have Christmas lunch at the restaurant again this year, it's so much easier with all of us and we can easily fit in extra people, especially if they have nowhere to go. We can easily organise that. And then for the long term I will get a few people on the street together, with you as well and we'll get families to take someone in. Perhaps not every week, because that might be a bit much, but say twice a month to start with? Jon and I will definitely open our house to someone, as will Polly and Matt, Frankie and Tomasz will too, I am sure, then there are others.'

'You think we can make this work?'

'Yes, we'll start with your ten and who knows, we might get more people willing to help out as well.'

'Oh Claire, I can't tell you this means to me.'

'Meow,' George said.

'And George. You know we both felt that we needed to do something about people being lonely. I was so lonely not that long back, you know when Marcus and I fell out and

I was a bitter old man, but look at me now . . . It was George's idea as much as mine though.'

George purred.

'You should say that at our meeting, Harold, because it's perfect and yes look at you now. You've got a son, a nearly-daughter-in-law, a granddaughter and a new grandbaby on the way, not to mention all of us.'

'And Snowball, George and Alfie, and of course Hana too.'

'Woof,' Pickles said.

'You're a dog, Pickles,' Claire said petting him. 'I always include the animals when I say us,' she laughed. 'You know I was lonely too when I first met Alfie, a long time ago, sometimes it feels like another lifetime, but I do remember how it felt and I wouldn't want anyone to feel that way.'

'Me either, which is why I so desperately wanted to do this.' Harold had tears falling from his eyes.

'We'll make a brilliant team.' Claire hugged him.

'Meow.' I jumped on Claire's lap. Yes we would, Harold, Claire, George, Snowball and I. We would be the best team ever. And Pickles, he was part of our team of course.

Chapter
Thirty-One

We all turned up at Sylvie's house the usual chaotic mass of people. The kids were excited because it wasn't quite Christmas but it was close, Pickles was excited because since the chocolate incident he was back to usual. Jonathan had bottles in his hands, as did Matt, and Tomasz and Franceska turned up with food. It was so familiar. When Marcus came in with Harold and Snowball in tow, I realised that it was all as it should be. Apart from the fact that George and Hana had disappeared. Maybe this was my chance to find out what was really going on.

As everyone settled down to eat, I turned to Snowball.

'We need to go and find out if Hana and George are together, once and for all,' I said, sounding every inch the parent.

'How?' she asked.

'We need to spy on them and before you say it, I know it's an invasion of privacy but I really want to know.'

'Why don't you just ask him, Alfie?' Pickles said. I hadn't realised he'd been listening but I should have, as we were near the food bowls.

'I've tried, believe me I have. Follow me.' I headed upstairs and crept along the corridor to Connie's room. In there, curled up on the bed were George and Hana, looking very cosy.

'Right, keep quiet,' I commanded.

'There they are,' Pickles shouted, blowing our cover immediately. They sprung up as Pickles waddled over to them, his tail wagging.

'What are you doing here?' George asked.

'I could ask you the same, young man,' I replied.

'We were just having some time alone, Alfie, we weren't doing anything wrong,' Hana said sweetly, her eyes wide with worry.

'Of course you weren't,' Snowball said, shooting me a glance which meant I would be in trouble later.

'They were spying on you because they want to know if you are boyfriend and girlfriend,' Pickles explained. That dog was as subtle as a sledgehammer, as he spilt all my sleuthing beans.

'Why didn't you just ask?' George said.

'That's what I said.' Pickles sounded pleased with himself.

'I did, I've been asking you ever since we came back from holiday. I even tried to see for myself but I fell in a bush . . .' Oops, I shouldn't have said that.

'I am fed up of you invading my privacy,' George stormed. But then Hana laughed and Snowball laughed.

'Oh George, don't be cross. Firstly it's nearly Christmas, and secondly, at least you have a dad who loves you,' Hana said. 'Put him out of his misery.'

'Yes, put me out of my misery,' I reiterated. 'Please.'

'OK. I love Hana, but we're young and we don't want to rush anything. So yes, she is my girlfriend but we're taking it slowly.'

'We're being sensible, like Aleksy and Connie,' Hana explained. 'We're young and we have plenty of lives left in us.'

'Oh boy, I couldn't love the both of you anymore,' I said, leaping on the bed and nuzzling them both.

'Ahh, get off,' George said, but he was grinning.

'What about me?' We all laughed as Pickles jumped up onto the bed with us and licked us all.

Downstairs everyone was chatty. Food was eaten, we were given a few treats. Sylvie was smiling but in that way when someone is putting on a brave face and I knew she was going to miss Connie.

'So are you excited about Japan?' Matt asked her. She shot a worried look at her mum who just smiled.

'I am, I'm nervous about flying on my own. It's a long flight.'

'But they're going to take good care of you, I've made sure of that,' Sylvie reassured. 'And think you can watch whatever films you want without me telling you they're not appropriate.' She laughed a little and I was so proud of her.

'We'll all miss you,' Claire said. 'But imagine it will be such an adventure. And you can tell us everything when you get back.'

'I want to go to Japan,' Summer shouted.

'Do you know where Japan is?' Jonathan asked.

'No, but I want to go anyway.'

'Room in your suitcase, Connie?' Jonathan said, and everyone laughed.

'I couldn't be doing with it myself. All that flying in a big tin can, people everywhere and then all that funny food,' Harold said.

'Harold, I grew up there, the food is normal to me,' Connie pointed out.

'That might as well be, if I was you I'd pack some bread,

and some tea, in case you need to be reminded of home. I'll miss you, lass,' he said, softly. Connie ran and threw her arms around him.

'And I'll miss you too, Grandpa.'

'Grandpa?' Harold had actual tears in his eyes.

'You a bit emotional, Dad?' Marcus asked.

'Not at all just allergic to dust.'

We all knew there wasn't a spec of dust in Sylvie's house.

Aleksy and Connie went to the garden, and I followed them, but tried not to be obvious. I had asked Snowball to keep Pickles busy and she was, bless her, watching him chasing his tail, and asking him to do it again so she could do so. I wasn't sure if she would get bored first or Pickles so dizzy he'd fall over.

'I wanted to give you my Christmas present before you went,' Aleksy said, shyly. His cheeks were red as he handed over a bag.

'Oh Aleksy, I was going to give yours to your mum so it would be under your tree on Christmas morning.'

'And I'd love that but I wanted you to have this. We put a lot of thought into it,' he mumbled, looking at his trainers.

'Who's we?'

'I mean me, of course. Go on, open it.'

Connie pulled out a book, then a charm which Aleksy said was a St Christopher for keeping her safe on her travels. I have to admit I felt a little emotional. Then she pulled out a box. As she opened it she gasped. I shuffled nearer, so I could see. It was a silver chain with a letter 'C' attached.

'It's the most thoughtful gifts I've ever received, Aleksy, thank you.' She put the necklace on and kissed him. I knew

I shouldn't be watching but hey, Aleksy was one of my first protégés, and my boy had done well. I was proud of him.

'I love you, Connie and I want you to have a lovely Christmas. But don't forget about me,' he said.

'Don't be silly, as if I could ever forget about you. And I'll bring you back something cool from Japan.' She paused. 'Make sure my mum's OK won't you? I know she's got Marcus and the baby bump but we've never been apart at Christmas before.'

'I will, I'll take care of her too. We all will, and when you come back we'll all be together again and soon the new baby. We could be the babysitters for them.'

'I'd like that, thanks Aleksy.'

My heart was fit to burst.

Everyone burst into the back garden.

'Are we interrupting?' Polly asked.

'No,' Aleksy said. Connie blushed.

'We just thought that it would be nice to have a photo, you know all of us, the whole family.'

We were organised, the humans gathered us up in their arms – Pickles by Henry, Toby insisted on holding George, Snowball sat on Harold's lap, he'd been placed on a garden chair and Claire had me in her arms. Hana of course was with Connie. Marcus set up a tripod and a camera which he put on a timer.

'Say "cheese",' he said.

'Cheese,' everyone said.

At the mention of his favourite food, Pickles jumped out of Toby's arms and landed on Snowball, who was on Harold, Snowball squealed and then jumped, but was luckily caught by Sylvie. Everyone turned their heads just as the camera went off.

'Perhaps next time we should say a non-food related item,' Polly suggested.

That night, Snowball, George, Hana – who had decided she would brave the cold to hang out – and I sat in our back garden.

'It's been eventful again, hasn't it?' I said.

'It's been such a crazy time for me,' Snowball said.

'We are happy and sad, aren't we?' Hana pointed out. 'That seems to be how life works. We get happy, we get sad, and so on.'

'You're very smart, Hana,' George said. 'Almost as smart as me.'

Snowball and I tried very hard not to look at each other.

'But look at us, we have each other,' I said. 'And we have so many people we love around us.'

'Too many sometimes,' George said.

'No, son,' I replied. 'There will never be too many, because our hearts are so big we can love and love.'

'And that's what life should be about,' Snowball finished. We all watched the stars through the black sky in silence and I knew that at that moment we were all thinking about how lucky we were.

Chapter Thirty-Two

'So you want us to have an old person?' Vic Goodwin, Salmon's owner and the self-appointed head of the Edgar Road neighbourhood watch – along with his wife Heather, asked.

'Not exactly,' Claire replied. We had gathered some of our neighbours and friends in our living room. The Goodwins, Tiger's, or should I say Oliver's family, the Barkers, my main family and a family who lived next door to Harold that I wasn't familiar with. Harold had bravely invited them to come, although Claire was with him, as was Snowball. The children were all upstairs being looked after by Aleksy, Connie and Tommy.

'It was George's idea,' Polly said, with a giggle. I raised my whiskers. They weren't helping matters at all. I nudged George and told him to nudge Harold.

'You mean to tell me this was a cat's idea?' Heather Goodwin asked. The new couple, Carol and Steve, looked incredibly confused. The fact they hadn't run for the door was surprising, although in fairness, Tomasz, who was a big man, was pretty much stretched across it. We were all trapped.

'Oh dear Lord,' Jonathan said, rolling his eyes and glancing over at Matt who seemed to be finding it all terribly amusing.

George nudged Harold. He blushed, but cleared his voice.

'George inspired me,' he said. 'I know most of you know about my hospital time, and the fact that before my son and I sorted out a few differences last year I was on my own a lot.' Marcus went over and patted his dad on the shoulder.

327

'I've seen a lot of loneliness lately and I'm not happy about it,' Harold continued.

'It's a crying shame,' Mrs Barker said. 'No one should be lonely.' She had a tear in her eye. I went to rub against her leg and she looked at me gratefully.

'It is, and once a week I go to the senior centre which is a lifeline for us oldies, not so much for me because I am well looked after, but some there don't have anyone else. And in hospital some of the patients didn't have any visitors at all. So, Claire and I are going to go in once a week and see people, take them a cake, a smile, a newspaper and have a chat. It's like George did when I was in hospital.' Harold was on his best behaviour. He was also wearing his best suit because he told George he wanted everyone to take him seriously.

'I am so confused,' Steve said, glancing at the door.

'Never mind,' Tomasz told him, 'in about an hour it might all become clear. If not, there's lots of beer in the fridge.' This made him look even more confused, so Jonathan went to the kitchen and returned with a bottle for him.

'You see,' Matt said, deciding to take control a bit. 'Harold made a list of people who really are struggling with loneliness. Do you want to carry on explaining?' Matt said, as he got him back on track.

'Claire and I thought we'd launch a Sunday Lunch Club. We'd ask you, and perhaps you can ask your friends, if they would be able to host someone for lunch once or twice a month. At least they'll have somewhere to go, something to look forward to and a home-cooked meal, because some of them don't even have that,' Harold explained.

'I can't bear it, it's so sad,' Polly said.

'Right does that make sense?' Jonathan asked. He hated how these meetings could drag on and I know he was keen to sit down in front of the TV.

'What has it got to do with the hospital?' Vic asked.

'Nothing really, but that was where the idea originated. As Harold said, he and I will be doing some hospital visiting, but really we're looking for ten families at first to host Sunday lunch. What we can do is match you up with someone who is on their own, but you'd have to go and collect them and drive them home after as well,' Claire explained.

'So we do get an old person?' Vic asked, for the second time. I raised my whiskers, he was no spring kitten himself.

'Yes, you do. Now who is in?' Jonathan asked with a sigh.

'Of course,' Mr Barker said. 'We'd be happy, we don't go far ourselves most weekends, and we always have a nice Sunday roast, so we could easily have someone every week if they like.'

'We couldn't do every week,' Steve said. 'We go and see our kids you see, they live the other side of London, but definitely once a month to start with, then maybe more.'

'We're in,' Franceska said.

'I don't have a choice,' Jonathan mumbled but he winked to show he was joking.

When everyone in the room agreed to be a part of it, they also started suggesting other people who may help out too.

'I know, I shall make a spreadsheet,' Vic said.

'What's that?' Harold looked terrified.

'Come to mine, and I'll show you, we can make a spreadsheet of families who can host and then match them with people who need company, highly technical and very efficient,' Vic said, sounding efficient.

'Sounds perfect, Vic,' Claire said, giving his shoulder a pat.

We knew, as they carried on chatting, that we'd done it. If Vic and his spreadsheet were involved then it was now a reality. The Goodwins might be busybodies but their hearts were in the right places. I was very fond of them now, deep down.

I felt emotional as George and I went to see what the children were up to. We found them all in Summer's room, and Pickles dressed up as a ballerina. It wasn't pretty.

'What is going on?' I asked.

'I'm a girl. I like being a girl. I think I might be a girl rather than a cat from now on,' Pickles said, twirling inelegantly around.

Oh boy, I thought, but we couldn't help but grin.

Later that night when everyone had left, I led George out into the garden. It was time for a dad to kitten chat. I felt nervous but determined. There was really just one piece of the puzzle left.

'George, you know that Snowball is here to stay, now?'

'Oh yes, Harold loves her. And although she's still missing her family, she seems to be settling in quite well too. Dad, I'm sorry I was so mean when she first came, but you know, with your history I felt as if she was going to replace Tiger.'

'No one can ever replace Tiger, George, you really need to understand that,' I said, fiercely, looking at the dark night and hoping to see the brightest star, which was always her.

'I know that now but you know I really like Snowball. She's very cool and funny, and sometimes I feel guilty about how much I like her, because of my mum.'

'But she would want you to like Snowball. Tiger was the best of cats, she wouldn't want you not to be friends with Snowball because of her.'

'I know that, but it's not always rational, feelings I mean.'

'No, they certainly aren't. But, George, you know I loved Snowball very much before and in my heart she isn't replacing Tiger, but I have to tell you that I still love her.' I held my breath as I waited for his response.

'I know, I can see it. I'm not silly like Pickles you know.'

'How do you feel about that?'

'I feel the same as I feel about my friendship with Snowball. I feel that it's right, and good, but I also sometimes worry that wherever Tiger mum is she'll think we've forgotten her.'

'I know, I feel that too. But we will never forget her, the two of us will keep her memory alive, along with our other friends. But you know without Tiger I've been a bit lonely. Not in the way that Harold's friends are, who don't have anyone, but just you know in that way.'

'That bit of your heart way, you mean?'

'Exactly that. When did you get so wise?' I laughed.

'I had the best parents to teach me,' George said and we nuzzled.

'So I have your blessing, with Snowball I mean?' I asked.

'Yes, you do. I might find it hard, I can't pretend otherwise, but I want you to be happy and I think that's what Tiger would have wanted too.' Just then we looked up and saw the brightest star in the sky and it seemed to be winking at us. We blinked back.

Chapter
Thirty-Three

'It's the most wonderful time of the year,' George said, in his sing-song voice. He was incredibly excited because it was Christmas Day. Our favourite day.

'It is son. Happy Christmas.' We nuzzled.

It was early, of course, because our children woke at the crack of dawn, or so it seemed, to see if Santa had been. He had. As George and I watched them open presents, squealing excitedly about what they'd got, we felt warm and fuzzy. This was family at its best and it was also the scene that made it absolutely crystal clear how lucky we all were. We had so much, and it also made me spare a thought for those who didn't have as much, or anything close. We had to remember Christmas was about giving, receiving, and also being mindful of everyone else. What saddened me about the world sometimes is how people don't value people enough, or cats for that matter. Anyway, enough of my sad thoughts, because no one should be miserable on Christmas Day.

The run-up had been hectic, as it always is, although in a different way this year. Harold's Sunday Lunch Club was up and running, although it was very early days, and today we had five people dining with us who would otherwise be on their own for Christmas. And not only that, there would be no turkey for them if they didn't join us. I, for one, found that unimaginable because that was my favourite thing about Christmas. George also quite liked Brussels sprouts but I didn't quite understand that.

The Goodwins and the Barkers were having Christmas Day together, and they had invited three other people, which was kind of them. In the new year, the regular Sunday lunches would start properly, and Harold was very proud of himself. As was I. And of George, who inspired this whole thing. Claire was working with the Goodwins as well, to try to get more people involved. They were starting with Edgar Road, because it is a very long road, they felt they should be able to get many people to sign up. With the combined forces, I couldn't see how it would fail. Claire had the charm, Vic would talk until people agreed to anything and Heather never took no for an answer. We all had high hopes.

There had been the usual pre-Christmas fun of course. The nativity play which Toby, Henry, Summer and Martha were all in. It was pretty uneventful compared to last year when we put George in the manger as baby Jesus. People are still talking about that, and oh how I'd enjoyed it but we were absolutely banned from going this year. Claire even locked the cat/dog flap, she wasn't taking any chances as we were trapped in the house.

The Christmas tree had also managed to survive relatively unscathed, as George didn't climb it this year. He said he had grown out of that, but the same couldn't be said for Matt and Polly's because George taught Pickles to try to climb it instead. Pickles had gone back to trying to be a cat having abandoned trying to be a girl, and George showed that despite his maturity and his discovery of his purpose in life he could still be naughty. It didn't end well. Polly was furious as decorations scattered, the tree almost landed on Pickles, who thankfully escaped unhurt. We were all cross with George and even he realised he'd pushed it too far. He promised to act as a more responsible older cousin to Pickles but I wasn't holding out much hope on that. Thankfully Polly had the sense to ban putting presents around the tree, in case Pickles ate them and we had adopted that policy at our house as well.

I had been spending more time with Snowball and my other Edgar Road friends, now we had a little less going on. Snowball and I were back to being a couple, and although at times I did feel guilty about Tiger, I knew, deep down, she would want me to be happy. And I was happy. Some days I woke up and wondered how I was so happy, because since losing Tiger, I'd been far more down than even I realised, but it was as if I now had a new lease of life.

It was as if I was on life four of my nine lives. I had rediscovered a spring in my paws, which I never thought I would have again, and I felt invincible. I still thought of Tiger every day, and George and talked about her all the time, but it was finally time for me to move on, and as it was with Snowball, my first love, it made sense. If that made sense. But I wasn't replacing Tiger. I hadn't gone out looking for a new cat. I was back in love with someone I loved before.

George pretty much accepted it with good grace. He and Hana were closer than ever now he had stopped going to the hospital, but he also visited Snowball and Harold a lot. He sometimes would have a teenage strop and tell me that I better not ask him to call Snowball mum, but as I explained that would never happen, he was silenced. And he did really like her, they were pretty good friends actually.

So as we approached the end of the year, it was happy families, and love and laughter filled our lives once more. As did the fact we were helping people who might be lonely. What I loved about all our friends and family was that we all knew how much we had, so we were willing to make the lives of others better. And that is what life should be about. Sadly I know it's not, but it should be. That's how it would be if cats ruled the whole world.

The streets were pretty empty as a convoy of adults, children, cats and a dog made their way down the street on Christmas Day to go to Franceska and Tomasz's restaurant, so we only received the odd strange glance. Marcus had gone to pick up some of our new guests and Harold, as it was bitingly cold and too far for them to walk. Matt had also gone to pick up a couple of others as they couldn't all fit into one car. The children chattered excitedly, no longer fighting over Pickles' lead; that particular novelty had worn off a bit, and also they had all insisted on carrying one of their new toys with them. I couldn't wait. Not only was I spending Christmas Day with my favourite humans, George, Snowball, Hana and Pickles, I was also going to see Dustbin and Ally. Not to mention my turkey dinner. I really couldn't wait for that.

The restaurant was warm, welcoming, with lights twinkling everywhere. Frankie greeted us all with hugs and kisses, Tomasz was cooking, and Sylvie and Claire went to help him. Jonathan organised the children, while Franceska poured drinks. Tommy and Aleksy played a game on a tablet; rare for the brothers to share a moment together. I knew Aleksy was missing Connie, but it was nice to see them hanging out, and I hoped it would bring them closer together.

We cats skipped happily out the back to wish Dustbin a Happy Christmas.

'Well I never, it's Snowball.' Dustbin raised his whiskers in greeting. 'How lovely to see you after all this time.'

'Remember, George, I told you that I ran away once and Dustbin literally saved my life,' Snowball explained.

'Yes, but that was down to Alfie, really,' Dustbin said. We all spared a thought for our old memories.

'Isn't it great us all being here together?' Dustbin said as he introduced Snowball and Hana to Ally.

'Hana, come outside,' George coaxed, she was still stood just inside the door.

'But it's so cold on my paws,' Hana replied, tentatively lifting a paw out. 'Brurrgh,' she said, shivering. We all smiled at her fondly.

I went back inside when I heard Matt and Marcus arrive, as did George and Hana. Snowball stayed outside to catch up with Dustbin and Ally.

Harold proudly led our new friends, Les, Mary, Val, Jack and Alan in. I felt so proud and sad at the same time. I still couldn't quite come to terms with the idea that people were alone at Christmas.

'Thanks so much for having us,' Mary said, she was quiet and a little nervous. Our families had decided that they would share the old people, although Claire said we shouldn't say it like that, you know what Jonathan was like. However, this way us, Polly, Matt, Franceska, Tomasz, Sylvie and Marcus would make sure they were looked after and we'd somehow ended up with an extra person too, but it didn't matter because we had enough love to go round. George and I enjoyed the extra fuss we got when we saw them also.

I went to greet them all by rubbing their legs, but Alan

looked a bit shocked. He wasn't a cat person, and didn't make a fuss of us, but George and I had decided that we'd soon convert him.

'You are all so welcome,' Franceska said, 'now can I get you drinks. We've got Prosecco?'

'Oh I've never had it,' Val said. 'But I wouldn't say no.' She grinned. She had never had children and her husband died a few years ago, so she'd been on her own ever since.

'I think I might rather a sherry?' Mary said, sounding a little uncertain. I guessed we were overwhelming all together, and they weren't used to us yet.

'Meow.' I tried to reassure them all.

'I'd love a beer,' Jack said.

'We've got sherry, beer, wine or Prosecco, you're welcome to whatever you want,' Jonathan said, as he took orders.

'And can I take your coats?' Franceska asked, as they finally shrugged off their coats. Matt and Harold led them to the table.

'Take a seat,' Harold said. He was definitely enjoying taking charge.

'Is there anywhere we should sit?' Val asked.

'Wherever you like,' Harold replied. I watched as they levered themselves into chairs, just as drinks were delivered to them, and the children came over.

'We wish you a Merry Christmas,' Summer and Martha sang. They were so angelic, I wondered what they'd been bribed with. Aleksy, and Tommy shook everyone's hands like the polite older children they were growing into and Toby and Henry introduced them to Pickles. Although our guests were still a little bewildered, it wasn't long before they started to relax. Our families had that effect on people.

Sylvie sat down with them. She didn't have a big pregnancy belly yet but she tired easily and had to take care of herself and the unborn baby. We didn't know what we were having yet but we were all very excited about it. Especially Hana, who was looking forward to having new life in their house.

'So, I hope you're going to enjoy today.' She smiled. 'It's a little crazy when we're all together.' That was an understatement.

'I just never saw a family who went to a restaurant and took their pets,' Alan said, nervously. 'But I'm so happy to be here, I can't remember the last time I had a home-cooked Christmas meal.'

'Oh Alan.' Sylvie who was emotional, hugged him which seemed to shock him even more. 'I'm sorry,' she added as she wiped tears from her face. 'But my little girl, who is fifteen and not so little, is in Japan with my ex-husband. It's my first ever Christmas without her and I miss her so much.' Her tears streamed down her cheeks and Hana jumped to comfort her as did Marcus. 'Oh it's fine, she'll be fine and so will I but I feel so strange without her. You know this morning, we would always wake up on Christmas morning and open her stocking. I wish she was here, that's all. Sorry.'

'Don't apologise, it's not easy, Sylvie,' Harold said, squeezing her hand.

'Thanks, Harold, right it's Christmas, I will make sure we all have fun.' She wiped her tears away and then went to see if she could help anyone.

'I don't know if I explained to all of you,' Harold continued, taking his role of organiser of this wonderful thing very seriously. 'But this is Tomasz and Franceska's restaurant and they never open on Christmas, so it's more like going to someone's home. And the cats, well what can I say, they come everywhere with us more or less. I can highly recommend getting a cat if you're lonely by the way, it worked wonders for me.'

'Meow.' Snowball appeared and jumped on Harold's lap. 'But at our age, what if anything happened to us and we left them?' Val asked.

'You can rehome an older cat,' Harold explained. Goodness at this rate they would all have cats by the end of this meal. Although possibly not Alan.

'Ahh, no, Pickles, stop, Pickles,' Henry started shouting. We all looked over.

'What's going on?' Polly asked, appearing from the kitchen.

'Pickles just ate a Christmas cracker toy,' Henry explained as he tried to fish it out of Pickles' mouth. Polly grabbed him, and managed to get it.

'How on earth did he get that?' Matt asked, scratching his head. We hadn't pulled any crackers yet. The children all shrugged innocently.

'Let's do Secret Santa now,' Marcus suggested, cleverly changing the subject.

All the adults exchanged gifts and the younger children all helped deliver them. Summer wanted to deliver a gift when it was Martha's turn and although Martha was pretty laid-back, she got cross, and then Pickles barked.

'Summer, you all take turns remember,' Claire said.

'She never likes to take turns,' Toby explained. 'But, Summer, as it's Christmas, you can have my turn,' he added.

'Yay!' Summer hugged Toby and I felt a pang. My children were growing up to be like us too.

'Also, and I won't have any arguing, you will all take home

some leftover food please, it will help me out,' Tomasz stated, as he prepared to go and put the finishing touches to dinner. I know he meant our new guests, as we all had plenty, but it had been decided before to cook extra food and send it home with our guests, by letting them think it was just leftovers and we needed them to help eat it up. That was Harold's idea too. He said like him, a lot of them were too proud to admit being lonely, or to needing help. I had learnt, through Harold, to understand that. I was quite a proud cat myself, after all.

Lunch was wonderful. We cats all ate together. Pickles was kept away, because we all know about his strict diet, and I did feel a bit sorry for him. However, he was given some turkey so it wasn't all bad. As we ate, I enjoyed listening to the low hum of happy human conversation and laughter. Crackers were pulled, hats put on, drinks refreshed – Mary was a little tipsy, her cheeks flushed and she giggled like a young girl. The rest of our new friends were all relaxing, as they were made to feel part of the family. The children were behaving again, all getting along, under the watchful eyes of Aleksy and Tommy, and everyone was having a lovely time which was all that mattered. It was all that ever mattered to me, to see my friends and families happy.

It was all any cat could ever want.

Later, as the clearing up was underway, we all headed to see Dustbin for the last time before it was time to leave. I told George we should take Pickles with us, too, after all it was Christmas, and as the adults had begun to unwind – with the help of a few drinks – they weren't quite so vigilant with him.

'You can come too this time,' I said, and he happily waddled after us.

'Hello again, Pickles,' Dustbin said, having met him when he broke out of home and we were on the recreation ground for Tiger's anniversary. We introduced him to Ally.

'You're a funny looking dog, if you don't mind me saying,' Ally said as Pickles licked her.

'He does that, he licks everything,' George explained, and Pickles licked the window nearest to him to illustrate the point.

'I don't exactly mind you saying,' Pickles replied. 'But I am more cat than dog now, surely?' he added. 'After all I've been practising for such a long time.'

'You're probably about as much cat as you're ever going to be,' George said and I nudged him.

'Yay! I knew I could do it,' Pickles replied. 'It was nice to see you but I've got to go inside now, Summer has dropped a lot of food and it needs clearing up.' He waddled back to eat the scraps.

'He'll never really be a cat will he?' George said.

'It's unfortunate but a lesson of life, there's no dog or human as clever as a cat,' I pointed out. 'But don't tell Pickles that.'

'So another year drawing to a close,' Dustbin said.

'And it's been eventful,' I added. 'What with Pickles' arrival, then Harold, George and his job, and Snowball.' I grinned over at her. I still felt a flutter in my heart every time I saw her and I could barely believe that she was back with us. Back in my life.

'I was so upset that my family moved away, and that I

had to be rehomed but it's worked out pretty well,' Snowball said.

'Definitely for us,' George said sweetly.

'And I met Ally,' Dustbin said. 'Which made me see what all the fuss is about.' He looked down and I knew this was an emotional time for him.

'And I am still here,' Hana announced, putting a paw out to join us and shivering. George nuzzled her.

'We are so lucky to have each other aren't we?' he said.

'We are and if we learnt anything this year it's the importance of love, of helping people and of friendship. Being a friend is the best thing ever.'

'I like friendship,' Hana said. 'I never had cat friends before I met you guys and I am so lucky to have you.'

'For me to have met friends again, old and new, when I could have been so lonely is a miracle,' Snowball added.

'And I love all my friends, old and new, human and cat. It's part of my job after all,' George added seriously.

'Well I for one am glad I met you all,' Ally said. 'I can't believe how much friendship has changed my life for the better. Being a friend is the best thing ever!'

'Let's toast to friendship,' George said, raising his paw. He'd got that from the humans who did it all the time with drinks. We all put our paws up, feeling the warmth despite the freezing cold.

'And it's easy to be a friend when you've got a friend called Alfie,' Dustbin finished.

Catstrology

By Alfie the Doorstep Cat & Astrologer Jessica Adams

Introduction

Ever wondered how your cat's zodiac sign affects its personality? What sign is the biggest hunter, or the most likely to be a lap cat? Which is the most fond of its food, or the most loyal? How does the zodiac sign affect their character? Can it also explain favourite foods, toys, pastimes and temperament?

Humans are always reading their horoscopes. Claire, one of my owners, insists on reading her and her husband's stars almost daily, so I thought it was about time that we did the same for cats. I, Alfie, believe that star signs are as relevant to cats as they are to people, so I wanted to put together this fun guide to your cat's star sign. I am a Scorpio and as you will see when you get to read about Scorpios, it really does explain a lot about my personality. Therefore, I am a firm believer in Catstrology.

Astrologer Jessica Adams, whose horoscopes appear everywhere from *Vogue* Japan, to *Family Circle* USA, to *Cosmopolitan* Australia, is helping me to delve into how the zodiac affects your favourite pets. In our brief guide, you can learn how your cat's star sign can affect your cat's personality. Personally, I believe it's as fascinating as pilchards.

Your cat's star sign is either when they were born or when they were adopted by you – and as many of you know, adoption is like a rebirth for us cats. By reading our special guide, you can discover which star signs belong to the most independent of cats, the biggest divas, the silliest cats, and the cleverest.

Welcome to Catstrology, or as I also like to call it, Alfiescopes!

Aries

The Aries cat is one competitive cat. Watch out as they can be prone to pick fights with other cats; the Aries is a natural fighter and will take on dogs, humans – probably even a giraffe. The Aries cat is also a biter. They are not necessarily aggressive but they do believe in the natural order. They like to be top cat! So, for example, don't take an Aries to a cat show; they do not like coming second or, worse, third.

The Aries cat is athletic and a very fast runner who can go from 0 to 100 with ease. These cats are competitive and will run races with greyhounds. Tickle an Aries cat's tummy at your own peril as you'll get attacked. They are quite the hunter, and will always be able to take care of themselves. I also wouldn't recommend getting too close with mouse-on-a-string or fish-on-a-rod games because the Aries cat will thwack you a good one.

Aries is a masculine sign so even the prettiest little female Aries kitten can seem blokey. Aries cats will often look good in a red collar. And whatever the coat, spiritually, the Aries cat is a ginger Tom.

Perhaps the best thing about the Aries cat is that you

always know your place with them. They come first, you don't.

Taurus

One of the overriding characteristics of Taurus cats is that they definitely like their food. They are greedy pussy cats who put on layers for winter . . . all year around. They also have impeccable taste in food as they prefer human food to cat food, likely because human food costs more. They are salmon mad . . . Cheese crazy . . . And they can even say 'Brie' in meow-meow language. They save food for later as if it's money in a bank account. They're not great at sharing that food though, so don't try to make them.

The Taurus cat will also earn its keep – they are excellent ratters. They do tend to bring their trophies home through the cat flap in return for rewards, and, if this doesn't work (we know that with humans, our trophies aren't always appreciated), the Taurus cat will learn tricks to earn rewards as they believe in being paid for a job well done.

Taurus cats like cat shows – if they win – but can be awfully miffed if they miss out on the money. Basically, the Taurus cat expects to be well rewarded. They can also be possessive about their belongings, so don't take their toy catnip mouse or there will be consequences . . .

Gemini

Geminis are the cats that like to communicate most. They are definitely a chatty catty! They have a vocabulary of different meows and it's up to you, as humans, to translate them. They are very bright cats, who know how to say words like 'hello' and ask 'why?', even as kittens. Leave paint around and Gemini cats will step in it in order to leave paw print messages around the house. It's cat code for whatever you don't normally understand . . .

Geminis are also computer cats who, like many of us cats, insist on lying on the laptop or sprawling all over the keyboard. However, the Gemini cat will take it further: they like technology and are the zodiac sign most likely to end up as a YouTube star. One of their favourite things is watching other cats on the internet and they will try to talk back to them. Communicator, friend, and technology savvy.

Gemini cats can look as if they are in cartoons a lot of the time because they strike a pose. You can see a thought bubble coming out of their head – even when silent, they are communicating.

Cancer

Cancer cats are known for affection; they make pretty good lap cats. They are cuddle cats that know when you need someone, and will get close – all the way up to your face. Cancer cats are most likely to miss their mums, so when bringing them home, pay special attention to their needs.

They are sociable cats and get lonely by themselves, so they either need other cats in the household or, at the very least, toy animals to cuddle up to. The Cancer cat is always one of the family and will fit right in with whatever family they are in. They will end up as the star in all Christmas photos. They can also be clingy and love to ride around on human shoulders.

They often strike the crab pose of the Cancer zodiac sign when asleep, curled up with their front paws under their chin. Cancer cats are also patriotic; they go wild at the World Cup and will leap up when the anthem sounds – let them watch the Queen's Speech at Christmas and they will be very happy cats.

Just a warning though: Cancer cats do not like change. They dislike moving house and can wander back, so be aware. Otherwise, lavish your Cancer cat with affection and they will certainly do the same to you.

Leo

Leo cats are the rulers, or monarchs, of the house – and the garden. They walk tall with their tails in the air, like the Stray Cats song. The Leo cat is the original Disney Aristocat. Even the strays and adopted tabbies look pure bred. Every Leo cat has pedigree and lineage, even if they are mixed breeds. Every Leo cat will have a special someone in their family tree and their bloodline may feature exotic breeds. Your tabby today may have been part exotic ocelot once. Dignified, with fabulous posture, they have beautifully aligned spines. Treat them like royalty and you will be fine.

Leo cats have personalities to match their looks. They rule the roost and find it hard to accept that any other animal can be part of the household. Any newcomer will have to be taken down a peg, permanently. But once again, as long as everyone knows their place, they will get on famously with the ruler of the cats: the Leo. This goes for other cats, humans and all other animals. Even pot plants need to learn their place with a Leo cat.

Virgo

Virgo cats can easily become bored and need to be kept busy. A bored Virgo cat will drive you and everyone else crazy – even making messes purely so they can help clean up. Eventually, you will realise that they essentially want to accompany you to the office. This is why Virgo cats spread themselves over your laptop or sit deliberately in front of the screen – it is not because they are being difficult, but because they need to get to work. Give a Virgo cat a job and they will be the most productive cat you have ever seen. Give them nothing to do and they'll also be productive, but your house might suffer as a consequence.

The Virgo cat is intelligent, has great loyalty and commitment, and can be a bit of a perfectionist. They love cleanliness. Make sure you give your Virgo cat tasks to do and they'll be happy all day long. But beware – a bored Virgo spells trouble. Maybe get a mouse in?!

Libra

Libra cats can make enemies quickly. And any enemies made by a Libra cat can last for years. They have their very own Wars of the Roses going on across next door's rose bushes, with a rival cat. Think Salmon and Tiger and you might get the right idea. Sometimes the feud lasts so long no one can remember what triggered it. It's more of a grudge than a violent exchange so try not to upset a Libra cat and you'll be fine. They are loyal as long as they feel you deserve such loyalty. It's not a bad idea to spoil a Libra cat.

Libra cats can also engage in mock attacks as a form of flirtation until their love interest hits back. It doesn't always work, but then wooing other cats is not easy for any zodiac sign . . .

Scorpio

Scorpio cats are passionate about life and love. Scorpio cats like to get involved . . . both their own love lives and those of other people – and cats. They are not terribly good on their own, and are never single for long. As a result, they can get into complicated relationships – oh yes, we know that one. Nothing is ever simple in the life of a Scorpio cat. Life is never simple for a Scorpio.

Scorpios like to have the upper paw in any situation. It doesn't take long before they have humans or other cats wrapped around their little paws with their characteristic intense stare. Even when they are tiny kittens, Scorpio cats are very powerful.

Scorpio cats forgive and forget . . . not. They will find their own sweet way of exacting revenge if they feel they have been wronged by another cat, or even by you. It's about power: they need to make sure they still have it. But, in fairness, the Scorpio cat will always use that for good rather than evil, so it's fine. Mostly . . . Scorpio cats might be a little self-absorbed, but they definitely have their hearts in the right place. Their heads . . . well, that's another story.

Sagittarius

Sagittarius cats are the thinkers of the cat world. If there was a spiritual leader of cats, they would be a Sagittarius. These are philosophical cats – like T. S. Eliot's great thinkers and dreamers – and they have a benign smile on their face that might remind you of a Zen Buddhist or perhaps a monk from the Middle Ages. They've got it all figured out. With their incredible intelligence and calm manner, they can really understand what is going on.

Sagittarius cats also like to travel, even if only within their own universe. They will be out and about exploring a lot and learning from their environment. It's how they learn the meaning of life. And, as their owner, you will be able to see them thinking at all times. You might not know what they're thinking, but, rest assured, it will be very deep.

Capricorn

The Capricorn cat is one busy cat. This is the kitten who climbs up the curtain or clambers up to the top of the step ladder in the garden – no fear of heights here! Ambitious? Absolutely. Capricorn cats have a knack of getting to extreme heights and they feel quite comfortable there. It's reflective of their need to strive for the top in all things. They also feel no sense of danger so watch out as they might need to have that pointed out to them at times.

Perhaps the most determined of all the cat signs, Capricorn cats can also be very helpful and practical. You need to be careful that they don't get into too many scrapes – and, if they do, you need to be on hand to save them. Being the owner of a Capricorn cat can be very time-consuming, but there will never be a dull moment. And if you ever need help putting the fairy on top of the tree at Christmas, you know who to ask . . .

Aquarius

The Aquarius cat will be very popular – perhaps the most popular cat in the zodiac. The Aquarius is the only cat in town who will have a network of dogs, goldfish, parrots and other oddities in the neighbourhood. It's a gang, and what a gang! Aquarius cats like to know they are part of a greater animal tribe. Even hamsters can join . . . Very inclusive and welcoming, the Aquarius cat won't make anyone feel they don't belong. Even humans are fully included in their pack.

But Aquarius cats can also be very indecisive. Do not give them two bowls of food; the effort in trying to decide might be far too much for them. But, as a general rule, they are pretty easy going, fun to be around, and always ready for a party.

Pisces

The Pisces cat is away with the fairies. A dreamer, not a doer – and sometimes you will feel like tapping a Pisces cat on the side of the head to enquire if anyone is home. They love fish tanks and ponds, and can spend hours watching fish drift past. They will be constantly curious about your bath or shower and will try to get in. They don't necessarily share the normal cat fear of water.

Pisces cats like to go under objects – particularly beds, but also garden sheds, so be careful. They love hiding, so you might find them under chairs and tables too. Their disappearing acts will start as soon as you get them home, even when they are tiny kittens.

The Pisces cat is also sensitive. They have beautiful, almost liquid eyes. They are psychic and know when you are going away or coming back, so it is no coincidence when you find them waiting for you at just the right time . . .

One ordinary neighbourhood.
One extraordinary cat.

Read the *Sunday Times* bestseller and find out how it all started. The tale of one little grey cat and his journey to become a Doorstep Cat.

They were a family in crisis.
He was a friend for life.

Read the follow-up to the smash-hit bestseller,
Alfie the Doorstep Cat.

One little kitten.
A whole lot of trouble.

The *Sunday Times* bestseller returns –
and this time he has a sidekick!

It's time for Alfie's first ever holiday!

The *Sunday Times* Bestseller
RACHEL WELLS

ALFIE
The Holiday Cat

Alfie and George are back for more adventures – this time taking them a long way from home . . .

Can Alfie and George save Christmas on Edgar Road?

The *Sunday Times* Bestseller

ALFIE
In The Snow

A family in need. An extraordinary cat.
A time for miracles.

RACHEL
WELLS

**Another heart-warming Alfie
adventure that is perfect to curl up
with this festive season.**